CW00971756

EASTBOURNE'S GREAT WAR
1914-1918

R A Elliston

S.B. Publications

By the same author

Lewes at War 1939-1945

Brighton's Tram Days

Published by SB Publications
19 Grove Road Seaford East Sussex BN25 1TP

© Copyright R A Elliston 1999

All rights reserved

No part of this publication may be reproduced, stored, or transmitted by a
form or by any means electronic, mechanical, photocopyin
recording or otherwise without prior permission of the copyright own
and the publisher.

ISBN 1. 85770 146. 1

Printed by
Adland Print Group Company Limited
Unit 11, Bellingham Trading Estate, Franthorne Way,
London SE6 3BX
Telephone: (020) 8695 6262

CONTENTS

Acknowledgements
About the book and the author
Dedication

<u>Front Cover</u> :	Return to the trenches
<u>Back Cover</u> :	A silk postcard of the Royal Sussex Regimental badge: a souvenir from the trenches.
<u>End Pages:</u>	Peace Day Programme and War Certificate

ILLUSTRATIONS

Blue Boys on Excursion from Summerdown Camp

ABOUT THE BOOK

This is a very welcome addition to the collection of books on Eastbourne. Of the many volumes which have appeared over the years this is the first to deal exclusively with the 1914-1918 war and to give in-depth details of life in the town at the time. At this distance in time from the period, very few people now have any recollection of the events themselves and have only heard reminiscences from older relations, friends and acquaintances.

Bob Elliston started his researches some years ago on the Admiralty named Polegate Airship Station (actually in Willingdon Parish). This study was followed by a widening interest which eventually covered every aspect of war- time life in and around the town amongst both the armed forces and the civilians. The official records in various repositories and collections throughout the country have been diligently searched for information, newspapers scanned and abstracted, people interviewed, photographs secured and maps and plans consulted.

I hope that reading this volume will help bring back to us over 80 years on recollections of what we owe to the men and women who fought the war abroad. It will also give a greater appreciation of what it was like for those who remained at home. It contains so much about the period that it should become a point of reference for years hence.

Vera Hodsoll, Eastbourne Local History Society, August 1999

ABOUT THE AUTHOR

R A (Bob) Elliston is a Brightonian who apart from a spell in London has spent his life in Sussex. After a career in hospital pathology, he retired from the Eastbourne Health District Laboratories and has since devoted his time to local history specialising in aspects of the World Wars amongst other topics. His father, Charles Arthur, served with the 13th Battalion Royal Sussex Regiment (Lowther's Lambs) from 1915-1918 No SD3505.

ACKNOWLEDGEMENTS

This book could not have been written without the help of the following so readily given.

The staff of the Eastbourne Reference Library
The staff of the East Sussex Record Office, The Maltings, Lewes
The Librarian of The British Red Cross Society London
The Imperial War Museum London
The Maritime Information Centre Greenwich
The Royal Air Force Museum Hendon
The Fleet Air Arm Museum Yeovilton
Maps reproduced by kind permission of the Ordnance Survey, Southampton, Licence No MC99/286
The Royal Aeronautical Society
Mr Martin Brown, East Sussex County Archaeologist
The Librarian Richmond Reference Library, Surrey
The Aust-Agder Muset, Arendal, Norway
The War Museum of Military History, Saxonwald, South Africa
Mr Peter Bailey, Newhaven Maritime Museum
Mr Keith Fuller, Curator, Sussex Yeomanry Archives
Mr Geoff Bridger, Mr Julian Sykes and Mr Terry Whippy, of the Western Front Association

Members of the Eastbourne Local History Society in particular Miss Vera Hodsoll, Mr Ken Bathom, Mr Ted Hide, Mr Lou McMahon, Mr Michael Ockenden, Mr Michael Partridge, Mr John Palmer and Dr S J Surtees.

Residents of Eastbourne including Miss S Steer, Mrs D Collins, Mr Gordon Clark, Mr and Mrs Peter Ells, Mr Alan Green, Mr A Knapp, Mr M Knapp, Mr Dave Lester and Mr Philip Parker.

Mr Peter Howell for help with Seaford camp. Mr Leslie Stuart for aircraft and airship illustrations. Mrs Jean Thomas of Lewes for naval information.

The Museum of Shops Cornfield Road Eastbourne for ephemera

My gratitude to my granddaughter Joanne Armstrong for editing the maps, my daughters Jane Armstrong and Ruth Rowland for correcting the typographical errors and to Miss Vera Hodsoll for saving me from the worst of my failings in scholarship and local history.

DEDICATION

By the Millennium the few survivors with adult memories of the events of the Great War or World War One (1914-1919) as it is now known would have to be centenarians. The date is not a misprint the 11th of November 1918 was an Armistice, peace was not secured until the signing of the Treaty of Versailles in June 1919. It was a war which claimed the lives of 1,056 men and women of the town. Historians are already regarding the two great world wars of this century as connected events, in fact a second "Thirty Years War". This book is a record of the sacrifice and effort of the town and its people in a stand against aggression in which a war was won and peace lost.

1. THE LAST DAYS OF PEACE

The first years of the twentieth century were marked by intense competition in Europe between the principal powers for economic and military supremacy. An arms race between Germany and Britain to build more and more warships had gathered momentum. By 1914 the allies had over 40 battleships to Germany's 20. Germany had increased the size of its standing conscript army, the cost of which coupled with its naval expansion placed severe financial constraints on that country. Germany sought to become a world power and was a latecomer in acquiring an Empire overseas. Britain's economy was the strongest in the world whilst Russia was the world leader in industrial expansion.

After 43 years of European peace following the Franco Prussian war Germany had forged alliances with the Austro-Hungarian Empire and Italy to create the Triple Alliance, later referred to as The Central Powers. By 1907 France, Russia and Britain had concluded agreements to support one other known as the Triple Entente and as this grouping enlarged it changed its name to The Allies. The seeds of conflict were sown, and each nation had its own reason for going to war. The Austrians to teach the Serbs a lesson, the Russians to support the Serbs. The French to regain Alsace-Lorraine, and the Germans goaded by a fear of encirclement to seize a window of opportunity to succeed before Russia outperformed them. In Sarajevo on 28th June 1914, a Serbian student, Gavrilo Princip fired the fatal shot at the Austrian Archduke Franz Ferdinand. This precipitated the chain of events which led to war. Following Germany's attack on Belgium and France, Britain's guarantee of Belgium's neutrality brought this country into the conflict on 4th August 1914.

The self-governing countries of The British Empire, Canada, Australia, New Zealand and South Africa together with the imperial ruled colonies rallied immediately to support the mother country by declaring war on Germany.

In the high summer of 1914 Eastbourne went about its business in an untroubled way. A successful Sussex Agricultural show had taken place in June on a 12 acre site on the west side of Summerdown Road. Guests staying at the Queen's Hotel had complained of the noise from seaplanes from the Eastbourne Aviation Company landing on the opposite beach. Those same guests would have had a grandstand view of the arrival of the 1st Battle Squadron of the Home Fleet on 1st July. The ships

Visit of the 1st Battle cruiser squadron Home Fleet *(John Palmer)*

anchored off the Pier and local boatmen were kept busy with trips to the fleet. Pier tolls amounted to £294 with 15,000 passing the turnstiles. The Corporation entertained the Officers of the fleet to lunch in the Town Hall and the ratings were refreshed at the Winter Garden, the cost to the ratepayers for the hospitality amounted to £117! A fête took place in Devonshire Park and a water polo match was arranged.

The British Red Cross had received its Royal Charter in 1909. Among the responsibilities with which it was charged was that of rendering assistance to the government in time of war. In June the three British Red Cross local detachments together with units from Hailsham, Westham and Heathfield held a field day in the grounds of Compton Place to practise treating the wounded in time of war. The Eastbourne College Cadet Force provided an attacking force and casualties, whilst the Church Lads Brigade helped set up the ground. Tents and marquees were erected and labelled Hospital, Advanced Dressing Station and Casualty Clearing Station. A feature of the exercise was a wagon loaned by the Duke of Devonshire's agent, Mr Roland Burke, which had been converted to a makeshift ambulance to convey four stretcher cases.

Red Cross improvised ambulance

The ground had been made available by the Duke, the Duchess and their daughter Lady Maud Cavendish were in attendance, also present were the Red Cross local President, Mrs Rupert Gwynne and the Mayor and Mayoress, Cllr and Mrs C W Bolton.

The local newspapers, the Eastbourne Gazette and the Eastbourne Chronicle kept visitors and residents informed of all the happenings in town. Each week a list of fashionable visitors was published giving details of arrivals, place of residence and members of each entourage including nurses and governesses in the party. No one could have foreseen that within a space of a few weeks that lists in the papers would be of wounded soldiers arriving for treatment in the auxiliary hospitals and more poignantly lists of local men who had been killed at the front.

The town mirrored the social conditions of the period the gulf between the living conditions of the upper classes and lower classes was marked.

Affluent Eastbourne's church parade on the western lawns

The well-to-do could afford to stay in hotels, and when at home were looked after by significant numbers of domestic staff, and provided that they had sufficient wealth led a carefree existence. Eastbourne stretched from Meads in the west to Royal Parade in the east. Inland Old Town reached as far as Summerdown Road and Victoria Drive. Ocklynge ended in Willingdon Road near Eldon Road. Green fields separated Hampden Park, Langney and St Anthony's from the town. Roselands contained many of the smaller homes of the working classes, builders, shop workers, laundry girls and domestic servants whose existence depended on servicing the needs of the affluent.

Most of the poorer homes were rented producing small yields for the landlord. This made repairs uneconomic so the living conditions left much to be desired. The Artisan's Dwelling Company had provided some social housing. In 1913 the Corporation purchased two sites, one in Victoria Drive of six acres and the other in Seaside from the Duke of Devonshire under the Housing of the Working Classes Acts and proposed to build homes for renting. Four years of wartime building restrictions would lead to an acute housing shortage by 1918. It would be difficult to match the call for "Homes Fit For Heroes". The Victoria Drive site would be commandeered for army use in 1916 on which was built a hutted camp known as the Cavalry Command Depot. These huts were taken over by the Corporation in 1919 to ease the acute housing shortage but were a far cry from what was expected by the demobilised soldiers and their families.

The Old Town Cinema workplace of CSM Nelson Carter VC

2. WAR DECLARED 4th AUGUST 1914

Men of the 2nd London Division of the Territorial Army in camp at Whitbread Hollow returned hastily to London for mobilisation. The Redoubt Fortress was used to accommodate 50 Naval Reservists, these

Ordnance Yard Seaside the town's main military base

would be joined by another group from Hastings and together they left under sealed orders for Brighton on a special train. At the Ordnance Yard in Seaside new recruits could be seen undergoing drill instruction.

The 4th battery Royal Horse Artillery of the 2nd Home Counties Brigade returned from their summer camp to the Drill Hall in The Goffs. They would soon proceed to Dover for embarkation. The unit was destined to serve in India and Mesopotamia. They were to be welcomed on arrival at Bombay by Lord Willingdon the Governor who was later to become the Viceroy of India.

The 490th Field Company Royal Engineers, a Territorial Army unit based at the Ordnance Yard, were on manoeuvres on Salisbury Plain at the outbreak of war. They returned in the early hours of 4th August to

Eastbourne for mobilisation. The unit left for Dover the next day to work on local defences. Then followed a period at Wingham in Kent for re-equipping and for receiving drafts of recruits. They left Canterbury by train on 21st December for Southampton and France, serving on the Western Front with the 8th Division throughout the war. Sixty men were lost and 150 wounded with a similar number being invalided out of active service. The unit returned home in 1919.

A call for horses for the army was made and 70 were requisitioned at the Ordnance Yard. Chapman's carriage proprietors, W H Smith, Pratt's Motor Spirit Company, grocers such as Cave Austin, Elliott's and Ridgeway's all surrendered horses to the army. The following week an urgent appeal was made for sets of harness. Only 150 sets of harness had

Artillery of 2nd Home Counties Brigade pass the site of the Picturedrome

been donated for 1,500 horses and more were needed from horse owners to make up the shortfall. Patriotism manifested itself with Sayers the boatmen offering their motor boats to the Admiralty whilst Mr Lovely, garage and taxi proprietor, of Cavendish Place offered the War Office 23 cars. Miss Galway of Meads gave an ambulance, which was supplied by

Caffyn's, for use by the Army in France. It did much useful work but spent its entire war at Bulford Camp on Salisbury Plain! Mr Lovely of the Cavendish Place garage offered a secondhand Buick chassis if a donor would defray the £200 cost of the ambulance bodywork. Caffyn trumped his ace by giving a complete ambulance free of charge whereupon Mr Lovely had to follow suit.

Requisitioned horses at the Ordnance Yard

The Eastbourne Borough Police Force lost 20 members called back to the colours as reservists. The Borough Accountant, together with five council officers and 20 workmen, also returned to the services. Seven firemen and 33 members of the bus department's staff rejoined the army. Six new three ton Leyland buses were requisitioned by the army but ten new ones had been ordered. The Council decided to make up the pay of all the reservists and volunteers who joined the forces. It was agreed that Territorial soldiers in uniform should travel free on the buses.

Home security exercised the minds of the authorities, the speed of the German advance through Belgium prompted fears of a seaborne invasion. A special committee to deal with arrangements if an invasion should occur was set up and remained in being until February 1919. The invasion notion persisted throughout the war leading to a significant number of troops being retained in this country. Aliens of Austrian,

German and Hungarian nationality were required to register with the police, failure to do so incurring a £100 fine. Internment of aliens followed shortly afterwards.

Dedicating Ambulance at the Pier

Pictured in the Eastbourne Chronicle under the heading "Prisoners of War" five Germans and one Hungarian were shown being marched down Grove Road under armed guard to the station en route to Horsham for detention. Anti-German hysteria manifested itself in letters to the newspaper about some Germanic street and house names in the town but subsided when it was pointed out the offending names had Scandinavian origins.

Mrs Davies-Gilbert placed Manor Hall, Borough Lane at the disposal of the Red Cross for use as a recreational and rest centre. The Red Cross War Hospital Supplies Depot at 20 Upperton Road, latterly the site of Private Patients Plan offices, launched an appeal for clothing for soldiers' shirts, socks, underwear and pyjamas, strangely requesting the items as being suitable to fit men six feet tall.   In September 1914 the first wounded British soldiers were seen in the town, they were on a day trip from Brighton. The men were from the Coldstream Guards, Highland Regiments and the Royal Artillery, some of whom had suffered facial injuries.   According to the report the men were being treated in

"Makeshift" hospitals. Soon Eastbourne would also have six of these "Makeshift" hospitals which, as elsewhere, would render sterling service.

On 15th August Mr Rupert Gwynne of Folkington Manor, the local MP, called for volunteers for the National Defence Force. Five hundred men were needed. Applicants had to be 35 years of age and over so as not to compete with army recruiting, they would be given an armband but

Kitchener volunteers in camp at Cooden

would have to provide their own uniforms and weapons. The uniform would be a waterproof Norfolk green jacket, green corduroy trousers and a slouch felt hat. This force would also be referred to as the Voluntary Training Force (VTC) and would enjoy an uneasy relationship with the War Office, tolerated but independent and not always ready to comply with official dictates. As the war progressed the authorities grudgingly accepted the contribution such forces would make in guarding public utilities and coast watching. This force would have similarities with the Home Guard of World War Two. The Eastbourne detachment had its headquarters at 81 South Street with Rear Admiral C H Harris of Grassington Road, as its commanding officer. By 26th August 270 had enrolled, drill practice was carried out in Larkin's Field (Saffrons), and

Eastbourne College grounds. Rifle practice took place on the Crumbles range.

The VTC guarded the waterworks and Friston reservoir with additional volunteers coming in by special bus from Hailsham and Herstmonceux. The cost of the guard was shared by the Eastbourne Water Company and the Council. The force served throughout the war finally being stood down in July 1919. The local Boy Scouts had been coast watching at Beachy Head for two weeks, the cost of refreshments for the boys amounted to £7. This was more than the council would tolerate so the Scouts' bun feast came to an abrupt end. The Scouts continued with duties at the Coastguard station where in January 1915 they were inspected by Colonel, later Lord, Baden Powell, the Chief Scout.

Public broadcasting and television had yet to be invented so war news was available only through local and national newspapers or by word of mouth. It was arranged that important events received by telegraph would be posted at specific points in the town, namely the newspaper offices; Town Hall, Bradford's Dairy, Carlisle Road, Howard's Stores, Green Street, at Hampden Park and, at the Crown, Hailsham.

Lord Kitchener did not share the view that the war would be over by Christmas. On 15th August he made his famous appeal for 100,000 volunteers to join the army for three years, or for the duration of the war. Nearly one million men responded to his appeal overwhelming the military authorities' resources. These men were to supplement the small regular force which had been sent to France. Over 4,000 local men volunteered, some from a sense of adventure and some as a way of escaping from the hardship and poverty which was then so commonplace. Many would be sent to Cooden under canvas and to billets in Bexhill. Eastbourne began to receive large numbers of men from Welsh, Border, and Lancashire regiments who had previously been housed in halls and private houses in Lewes.

These volunteers for Kitchener's third army had been placed in the 65th, 66th and 67th Brigades of the 22nd Division and had been sent to the South Downs for training. Some were under canvas at Shoreham and Seaford whilst others were in billets in Lewes, Eastbourne and Hastings. The tented camps became unusable due to the extremely wet autumn of 1914. Men who had originally been in Lewes and had moved to Seaford in October had to be housed in Eastbourne until March 1915.

In September, 2,600 Loyal North Lancashire and Manchester Regiment recruits arrived in the town for billeting. Later in December 1,000 men of the Shropshire Light Infantry, Cheshire Regiments and the South Wales Borderers arrived. They had been accommodated in two large tented camps at Seaford which were located on either side of Chyngton Road. These could house 10,000 men. Until the tents could be replaced with huts, private billets would be required. The Shropshires were placed in Old Town, with the Border Regiment in Meads, the Manchesters found homes in the Devonshire Park area. Roselands took the Loyal North Lancashires while the Cheshires were housed in the lower Meads area. A brigade sick room was set up in Blackwater Road Presbyterian Church hall with an army doctor, Red Cross nurses and RAMC men in attendance. As many as 200 men were seen each day so great was the activity that it was newsworthy to report that a telephone had been installed. The Loyal North Lancashire battalion was presented with a Nubian Goat as a mascot. The presentation taking place outside the Leaf Hall which was used as an Orderly Room.

The method of selecting homes for billets was direct, an army officer accompanied by a Police Constable would call on every house in a road. A few questions would be asked of the occupier about the number of rooms and occupants normally living in the house this being sufficient information for the officer to decide on the number of men to allocate for billeting. This often doubled the number of occupants with scant regard for beds, bedding, space or facilities. A householder who refused would very quickly be before the court as in the case of Mr Butcher of Ratton Road Ockynge who despite special pleading was fined £2 for his "Wilful refusal to accept three soldiers". The cover all " Defence of the Realm Act" enacted on 8th August 1914 enabled the government to impose measures at will on the population which allowed the foregoing prosecution to proceed.

Hotels and Boarding Houses would also be used for billeting. The York House Hotel was served with billeting papers on two occasions. The first was in December 1914 when 35 men of the King's Liverpool Regiment were placed there, the order excluding horses from the accommodation requirement. In November 1915, 33 men of the 2/5th Battalion of the Royal Sussex Regiment were housed in the Hotel, on both occasions the term was until further notice. The billeting papers contained instructions regarding feeding the men. Breakfast was to consist of six ounces of bread, one pint of tea with sugar and milk and four ounces of bacon. For a hot dinner one pound of meat eight ounces each of bread and potatoes or other vegetables and one pint of beer were specified. Supper was to consist of six ounces of bread, two ounces of cheese with one pint of tea. When horses were accommodated they had to be given ten pounds of oats, twelve pounds of hay and eight pounds of straw.

One of the Lancashire men who was placed with a family in Eshton Road, when his battalion departed to Aldershot, left behind one of the wooden clogs he had been wearing. It was a northern tradition that one would always come back to reclaim the clog, but sadly he never returned and the clog is now in the Towner Museum.

Preliminary training for the men consisted mainly of drill instruction, physical training, sports events and route marches. Evidence exists today in aerial photographs of complex trench systems dug for training purposes near the South Camp at Seaford and on Dittons Farm Polegate which replicated those found on the Western Front in France complete with zig-zags and saps. The Polegate trenches were ploughed out during the World War 2 food production drive. The men left Eastbourne in

The North Camp at Seaford (Peter Howell)

March 1915 for Seaford. In May seven trains were needed to convey the Lancashire battalions from Eastbourne to Aldershot and by November they were in France en route for Marseilles, Salonika and Macedonia.

The Local Government Board also asked the council to set up a "Relief of War Distress Committee" whilst the Board of Agriculture and Fisheries appealed to horticulturists to distribute spare seedlings to allotment holders to use for autumn sowings. Meanwhile in September the Council discussed band arrangements for the following 1915 summer season with the Devonshire Park Company. It was agreed that a uniformed band of military type with 31 players of first rate quality be engaged under an efficient conductor, summer concerts to total 25 and the winter to be 21. The Devonshire Park Orchestra of 25 to 31 players would give symphony concerts. The Council would pay half the cost of £7,336 and the Municipal Orchestra would be given notice to quit. A further £300 would be paid to Territorial Army bands for concerts in the Royal Parade bandstand. Total war had not arrived, but by the summer of 1915 the Territorial Army bandsmen would be too busy in France stretcher bearing to perform seaside band concerts.

Before 1914 wars were something for the small regular army to deal with, they took place at a distance, with few casualties and little disturbance to the life of the nation. Despite the terrible losses to come, the shortages of commodities and rising prices, war was still remote for many. It would not be until 1939 that the nation experienced total war.

Temporary Camps

Tented camps appeared in two locations in or near the town. One was at Spots Farm Willingdon the other at Horsey Bank. The record of their existence is sparse perhaps due to attempts to maintain security. The Horsey Bank camp near the junction of Churchdale Road (then known as Corporation Road) and Astaire Avenue (formerly Horsey Bank Road) came to light through a court case dated 4th October 1917. So far it has not been possible to determine the extent or occupation of this camp.

The local newspapers reported on 8th March that the King Edward's Horse a British unit attached to a Canadian Cavalry Brigade stationed at Maresfield Camp was expected in the town soon. In July of that year more definite news was received that the South Western Mounted Brigade were expected to be in camp at the end of Kings Drive near Willingdon village with Brigadier-General, the Earl of Shaftesbury, in command.

The Camp at Spots Farm was on Lord Willingdon's land having its entrance in Church Street, Willingdon at a point where it is crossed by the present A22 road. It was bounded by today's Willingdon Park Drive, Friston Avenue, Woodland Avenue and Willingdon Road. It provided a home for about 1,000 soldiers and the same number of horses. The men were under canvas whilst the horses were sheltered under corrugated iron canopies. The unit remained there until March 1916 when it was split up, some squadrons going to France and others to East Anglia.

On 1st September their arrival was confirmed when Leonard Peaty, a signalman of the Surrey Yeomanry, was fined 20 shillings with 9 shillings costs after a car collision. Any pretence of security was demolished following a newspaper report of a recruiting rally held on 6th October 1915 when the Earl of Shaftesbury took the salute, on Grand Parade, of the South Western Mounted Brigade. The band of Summerdown Camp played at the saluting base. The units comprising 1st Royal Wiltshire Yeomanry, 2nd Surrey Yeomanry, 1st Hampshire Carabineers, 1st Battery Hampshire RFA, 3rd Field Company Home Counties Engineers and the Brigades Mounted Field Ambulance. The parade formed up at Summerdown Road Camp and included the occupants of Summerdown Camp, in all about 2,000 men. Seven coaches from Chapman's, Contractors and Carmen, took those unable to march, the men of the South Western Mounted Brigade and 200 men of the 3rd (Reserve Battalion) Royal Sussex Regiment who had marched from Newhaven via Friston. The parade included an armoured car, general service and tool wagons, each drawn by four horses. Pack mules were also led in the parade. The route taken was Upperton Road, Grove Road, Silverdale Road, Grand Parade, Marine Parade, Seaside Road, Terminus Road finishing at the Technical School (Central Library) in Grove Road.

A series of minor accidents marked the South Western Brigade's stay. These included a collision with the wall of Langney Cemetery by a lorry of the Hampshire Carabineers, two lamp posts in Brassey Avenue and Brand Road knocked over by horse wagons of the 3/1st Signal Company Royal Engineers, all of which resulted in bills from the Corporation to the units.

The Seaford Camps

The tented camps at Seaford were located in the Chyngton area. The North Camp on land east of the cemetery, the South Camp between the Eastbourne Road and the sea. They were originally occupied by new recruits for Kitchener's army who had been housed in private homes and halls in Lewes and Eastbourne. The wet weather in the autumn of 1914 led to the tents being abandoned by the men. They returned to billets in Eastbourne in December until huts could be provided early in 1915. Later in 1915 men of the British West Indies Regiment were placed there but to their dismay soon became victims of an outbreak of mumps. Many of them died as a result and are buried in Seaford Cemetery. Later the camp was used for various Canadian Army units, Infantry replacement, Railway Construction and Engineers. Eastbourne was a regular place of entertainment for the men and those who needed medical care were sent to the 16th Canadian Stationary Hospital at All Saints Hospital.

3. LOWTHER'S LAMBS

On 15th August, Lord Kitchener Secretary of State for War called for 100,000 volunteers for the army. This was to supplement the small regular army and the Territorial force which had been sent to France. The Mayor took the chair at a mass meeting in the Town Hall on the 2nd September to meet the call. Colonel Claude Lowther, MP for Eskdale, Cumberland, who resided at Herstmonceux Castle formed a countywide committee of influential members of the community to raise a battalion of men for the Royal Sussex Regiment. A national "Rush to the Colours" took place in response to Lord Kitchener's appeal. In Sussex

Under Canvas Lowther's Lambs at Cooden Mount *(West Sx R O RSR3057)*

over 4,000 men had responded by January 1915 sufficient, with reserves, to form three battalions for the county regiment. A number of recruits came from outside the County, groups of Londoners and a number from a small village near Melton Mowbray testify to the activities of wandering recruiting sergeants.

The men who responded to Col Lowther's appeal were placed in three battalions of the Royal Sussex Regiment. Originally they were known as the 1st, 2nd and 3rd Southdown Battalions. They were embodied into the Army in May 1915 as the 11th 12th and 13th Service Battalions of the County Regiment with the 14th Battalion acting as a reserve unit.

Band of the 11th Battalion with Peter the mascot

The 4,000 volunteers all had the prefix "SD" to their service numbers. Later entrants would have general service numbers. They were known as the "Southdowns or Lowther's Lambs". In April 1914 an orphaned lamb from Mr J Passmore's, Applesham Farm, Lancing had been hand reared by the younger sister of one of the first batch of 50 Worthing recruits who had enlisted on 9th September, Lieutenant H L Frampton. This officer had just become engaged to the eldest daughter of the farmer. By November the lamb had matured sufficiently to be given to the Southdown Battalions as a mascot. The lamb "Peter" did not go to France and survived the war to be buried in 1928 in one of the rose beds at Herstmonceux Castle.

Each battalion had its own band with many bandsmen being recruited from the Salvation Army. Bandsmen also had the task of acting as stretcher bearers. Salvationists would have found this Samaritan role most worthy and entering the army also gave them an opportunity to spread the word. Local men were formed into separate companies for Eastbourne, Hailsham and Herstmonceux. These would make up the typical "Pals" battalions that would suffer so grievously on the Somme in 1916. Often men from the same firm would join up together as did 12 from Dickeson's and 23 men from Caffyn's.

The men all volunteers, as conscription was not introduced until 1916, would sign on at local recruiting offices throughout Sussex. Applications at Eastbourne could be made to A A Millward, Sussex County Cricket Club coach, of Cavendish Place, or at the Ordnance Yard. Many signed up at a special recruiting office opposite the station at 44 Terminus Road where Manns the estate agents are now located. After signing on and accepting the "King's Shilling", one day's army pay, the men would be medically examined. In the early days of the war this examination was of a perfunctory nature undertaken by a civilian doctor who would also be paid one shilling for every recruit passed and nothing for failures. In November 1914 100 recruits left the station for the 2nd "Southdowns" at Cooden Camp. On the 19th of the month the 1st Battalion visited the town by train on a recruiting drive marching to the Saffrons for a drill display and afterwards marched to the Ordnance Yard where they were divided into six sections for tea provided by a ladies' committee. A rally followed in Seaside Recreation ground. Evening recruiting concerts in church halls were a wet weather alternative.

Cooden Mount, a Victorian mansion with extensive grounds and the adjacent Belinda Farm at Sea Road, Cooden was owned by Mr Douglas Young, whose father, Alderman Henry Young was a London ironfounder. He offered the use of his grounds in which the Lambs could camp and train as his contribution to the appeal. The Kitchener appeal nationally had produced a million volunteers, ten times the number called for, completely overwhelming the army's resources. Conditions at the camp were primitive, bell tents for sleeping in, marquees for mess halls, wooden troughs and standpipes for washing whilst cooking was on field ovens in the open air. Few domestic items apart from those the men brought with them were available. No uniform, kit or weapons were to be had. Despite these shortcomings morale was high and basic training proceeded under NCOs who were mainly reservists.

The autumn of 1914 was particularly bad and conditions at the camp turned to a sea of mud. It was decided to build a hutted camp to accommodate the men and until these were ready in November the men were moved to the Drill Hall and the Downs School at Little Common Bexhill. The later recruits to the 3rd Battalion found themselves in billets in Bexhill. Whilst the men enjoyed these conditions the landladies were outraged by the War Office decision to pay a lower boarding allowance than was paid at Hastings or Eastbourne. This acrimonious dispute was not settled until after the Lambs had left the town.

With the huts completed, the first uniforms to be issued were known as Kitchener Blues, navy blue jacket and trousers with a forage cap. Equipment soon followed, leather belts, pouches and haversacks. The rifles were non-standard and thought to be of foreign origin although they looked good for drill purposes, they were unsuitable for firing. In early 1915 the long awaited khaki uniform with peaked caps arrived on which the Rousillion Plume badge of the regiment would be worn with pride. By Whitsun 1915 the battalions were embodied in the Army and at the end of June left Bexhill West Station for Maidstone and Detling Camp. Trench digging practice was undertaken with the construction of defences on the North Downs, a German invasion being considered a possibility.

The next move came at the end of September 1915 when the men left Detling for Aldershot where they were installed in the Malplaquet Barracks at the North Camp. This was a short stay before the men were moved into huts at Witley Camp on the main London Portsmouth Road.

Drummer simulates machine gun fire from wooden gun at Hooe

Here the "Lambs" would meet up with men of the 14th Hampshire Regiment, the four battalions now forming the 116th Infantry Brigade of the 39th Division. The first standard Lee-Enfield rifles were issued and musketry training followed at the Ash ranges at Aldershot. On the 4th March 1916 the brigade entrained at Milford for Southampton and thence by boat to Le Havre. A wintry scene of a tented camp above the harbour greeted the 3,000 men from Sussex. Soon they were in cattle trucks heading for the front line at Sailly-sur-Lys. The first fatality occurred on 12th March when Private David Dunk of Bexhill was shot by a sniper, thus the steady drip of casualties had commenced.

Front line duty alternated with periods in rest areas behind the front. The men were in the front line at Ferme du Bois, south of Richbourg on 30th June 1916. A set piece battle had been planned to straighten out the line of a German position known as the Boar's Head. The bombardment opened at 2.50 am and at 3.05 am the men climbed over the parapet and rushed the enemy's barbed wire and trenches. Smoke shells had been used to cover the attack, the smoke drifted about this causing in some places confusion amongst the attacking troops. The bombardment had failed to cut the wire, causing in some places the attackers to bunch together and present a good target to the enemy. The German front line was breached and attackers reached the third line but fierce counter attacks forced a withdrawal.

Company Sergeant Major Nelson Victor Carter, "A" Company 12th Battalion of Greys Road Eastbourne, distinguished himself in the action by despatching with his revolver the crew of a German machine gun and turning it on the enemy in so doing covering the retirement of the survivors. Later CSM Carter was fatally wounded in the neck whilst

bringing in the wounded. For his valour he was posthumously awarded the Victoria Cross his citation reading "His Conduct throughout the day was magnificent". The Council gave permission in October 1916 for cinemas in the town to hold benefit performances for the Nelson Carter Memorial Fund. By 31st July 1918 the fund had reached £472.

CSM Nelson Carter VC

Although the action lasted over four hours no ground was gained and the cost was grievous. The three battalions lost 349 Sussex men and 17 officers killed with over a 1,000 wounded, some of the casualties were returned to hospitals in Eastbourne. The lists of men admitted to the local Red Cross auxiliary hospitals contained the names of a number of the Lambs. Others went further afield to Scottish hospitals. The Southdowns had lost half their strength, hardly a town or village in the county escaped the tragedy. The Eastbourne papers in the weeks that followed carried lists of names of local men killed or missing.

A conservative count shows that 47 men from the town were killed that day. Edmund Blunden an officer in the 11th battalion in "Undertones of War" records a private soldier's comment on the day as "A butcher's shop".

The next day ten miles to the south the infamous battle of the Somme commenced which was to repeat on a much larger scale the failure and cost in lives of the Southdown's first action. During the whole of the war over 1,023 Lambs were killed in action, died of wounds or were posted missing. CSM Nelson Carter is buried in the Royal Irish Rifles Churchyard at Laventie south west of Armentiers. On that day 30th June 1916 in addition to CSM Carter's Victoria Cross, an officer was awarded a Distinguished Service Order, 4 others received Military Crosses. Eight Distinguished Conduct Medals and 20 Military Medals were awarded to other ranks.

After rest and reinforcements the Southdowns continued to serve and suffer. Festubert, Beaumont Hamel where the 11th Battalion suffered severe losses, Thiepval 1916, Ypres, Passchendale, St Julien 1917 and The March Retreat 1918. By May 1918 the 11th reinforced by men from other regiments were still a fighting unit and went on to North Russia in 1919. The 12th ceased to exist after March 1918 and the surviving few of the 13th were reduced to a training cadre on instruction duties with American infantry regiments

The War diary of the 13th Battalion makes sad reading for 25th November 1916 when it states that Private SD 4242 Reginald T---- was executed - shot at dawn. The sentence was carried out by fellow soldiers. On 21st October 1916 an attack had been launched on a German position known as Stuff Trench near Theipval on the Somme. It was here that the man failed in his soldierly duty, a previous conviction for disobedience weighing against him at Court Martial. The Division moved to the Ypres salient on 18th November taking their convicted man with them to his execution at Poperinghe where he was buried in the

New Military Cemetery. A brother of his and two cousins who all served in the 13th Royal Sussex were also killed in action

A poignant note was struck in a report of a meeting early in 1919 for returned Prisoners of War when Colonel Millward read the names of those men still reported as missing. Colonel Millward aged 29 was himself severely injured losing a leg after a shell burst near him during the March German offensive. After each name there was a pause in order that those present with information might speak. The comradeship which developed during the war carried on with reunion dinners at different places in the county until 1939. In 1974 the last reunion and memorial service took place at Cooden Mount, with a final dinner at Worthing in 1979 at which 13 of the few remaining survivors attended.

There was another VC holder who came from Eastbourne, Lieutenant Cyril Gordon Martin, of Grange Road. The officer had won the DSO in the retreat from Mons in 1914 whilst with the 56th Field Company Royal Engineers. He was in charge of a bombing party of six men on 10th March 1915 at Spanbroek Molen near Ypres. His task was to hold off an enemy counter attack which he did for over two hours and despite being wounded, he remained in action until ordered to retire.

4. THE RAMC AND THE ARMY HOSPITALS

The Kitchener volunteers were required for other corps in the New Armies as well as infantry. Eastbourne was chosen as a training location for the men selected to expand the Royal Army Medical Corps (RAMC). On 13th January 1915, 1,200 RAMC men arrived by two special trains to undergo ambulance and field emergency dressing instruction. They

The RAMC at Whitbread Hollow *(John Palmer)*

were accommodated at Cow Gap under canvas. Among the units formed were the 132nd, 133rd, and 134th, Field Ambulances which were later allocated to the 39th Division the same one that included the "Lowther's Lambs".

From newspaper reports it is known that three other Field Ambulance units were encamped at Whitbread Hollow the 65th, 72nd and 73rd. The local residents were assured by the press that they need have no qualms about the RAMC men as "they were recruited from men of good social standing". Proposals had been made to build a hutted camp in

Summerdown Road and to use the adjacent Workhouse as a training centre. On 24th March 1915, 3,000 RAMC men and 166 officers left Summerdown Camp for billets, many of the soldiers were housed in the Pevensey Road area and others in tents at Cow Gap. Amenities improved there when Earl Brassey opened a YMCA hut 150 by 30 feet at Cow Gap in June. In October a further transfer took place with 1,500 RAMC men billeted in homes east of Junction Road and to houses in Old Town leaving Summerdown mainly as a convalescent unit. In December 1915 the first RAMC contingents moved out to Farnham in Surrey for divisional training before going to France. Whilst the RAMC were at Cow Gap they made application to the Council to bathe at Holywell when the tide permitted. The Council refused insisting that they bathe at the prescribed times, but did agree to the men having reduced bus fares into the town on the Meads route.

In pre-National Health Service 1914 acute hospital services for the town were provided by voluntary hospitals. The Princess Alice Hospital in

RAMC in Kitchener Blues Summerdown Camp 1915

Carew Road had 62 beds, 24 of which were earmarked at the outbreak of war for wounded soldiers. The Leaf Hospital at 1-3 Marine Road had 20 beds, and although it started as a Homeopathic Hospital it also used conventional treatments and would play its part in treating war casualties. At the Ordnance Yard a military hospital of 16 beds had existed from as early as 1875. This was used for convalescent patients but from August 1914 until January 1916 it was the main military hospital for the town under Surgeon-Commander G S Robinson Scots Guards.

Central Military Hospital

The Eastbourne Union (Poor Law) Workhouse in Church Street, which later became St Mary's Hospital, was under the control of the Board of

Staff at the Central Military Hospital 1918 *(Dr S J Surtees)*

Guardians. Buildings occupied four sides of the site. These ranged from Napoleonic vintage barracks, through a Victorian infirmary, to the then contemporary offices, nurses home and a maternity block. A central open area was occupied by a parade ground, gardens and a chapel but this still left room later for the army to install twelve "Alywin" wooden huts sized 24 x 10 feet.

With the influx of Kitchener volunteers into the town together with the three Royal Naval Air Service stations, the need arose to establish a larger Central Military Hospital. The Guardians were given notice in July 1915 that the workhouse was to be requisitioned forthwith. The inmates were evacuated by 1st August, the healthy being sent to Hailsham and the sick to Steyning. The workhouse remained empty and in October 1915 the Guardians requested its immediate return, however by December Mr Roland Burke, the Duke of Devonshire's agent, was organising the conversion of the Workhouse to a military hospital. By January 1916 the first patients had been admitted. The hospital could accommodate 300 patients and had a staff of of 44 male nurses under a sergeant. The Matron had charge of eight nursing sisters and 25 VADs. The Voluntary Aid Detachment workers acted mainly as nursing assistants, many would have held Red Cross Certificates. Surgeon Major N H Mummery was the overall commanding officer.

16th Canadian General Hospital at All Saint's/St Luke's

The hospital was described as having 100 medical beds, 150 surgical beds and a block for infectious disease cases. The newly built obstetric unit was to be used as an operating theatre. The hospital remained open until July 1919 and during this time 16,000 service cases were treated. A memorial panel now at the Redoubt Museum commemorates the 100 patients and members of staff who did not survive. Fourteen were officers and 86 were other ranks. The men listed came from Australia, Canada and

South Africa in addition to the United Kingdom. Two women are named on the memorial, a sister of the Queen Alexandra's Imperial Nursing Service and a Red Cross VAD both of whom succumbed to influenza. Patients came from many sources the navy, the flying services and the army. Some would have been injured in road or flying accidents whilst on duty locally. Other cases were men sent back from France for longer treatment of wounds received in action. A further group would be local men sent for treatment near their homes for compassionate reasons.

The Canadian 16th Stationary Hospital

All Saints Hospital had been opened in 1869 by a charitable Anglo Catholic order to provide convalescent facilities for 150 of the poor of London. Additional accommodation was provided in 1890 for 100 children in St Luke's Hospital adjacent to All Saints. By May 1916 there were just 22 patients left in All Saints. Later that year these civilian patients were moved to Deerhaddnn an empty girls' school in Bolsover Road.

The Canadian 16th Stationary (Base) Hospital was established at the All Saints /St Luke's complex in January 1917 to continue the work of the Canadian 10th Hospital at Seaford which closed at the same time. There were few Canadian soldiers stationed in Eastbourne but the North and South Camps at Seaford could accommodate up to 13,000 men which would have produced a demand for hospital beds greater than could be met there. All Saints was fully equipped and staffed by the Canadians to take a maximum of 700 cases. It had an operating theatre, pathology and X-ray departments. It boasted ENT facilities, pharmacy, chaplain and "mental" department. Lt Col E Seeborn was in charge with 16 doctors, 27 nurses and 150 other staff. The Seaford camps were major Canadian training centres. Forestry Corps, Railway Construction battalions and Engineer units together with infantry units from across the whole of Canada provided patients. By October 1919 the unit had closed and left for home.

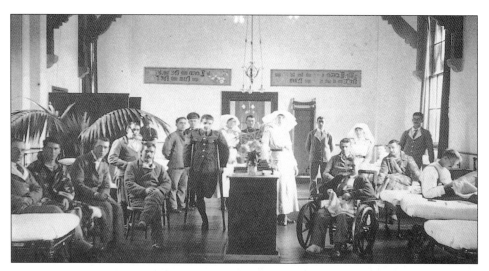

All Saints ward with amputee

Before its duties were finished it played a significant local role in dealing with the influenza pandemic of 1918. The 85 military personnel who died included 70 Canadian soldiers from the Seaford camps who were cared for at All Saints Hospital. Most of whom were returned to Seaford for burial. It would appear that of the 253 Commonwealth War Graves in the Seaford Cemetery 191 are Canadian and from details in the cemetery register, 114 were almost certainly influenza victims indicating that about 44 more died in the Seaford Camps from this disease. In most cases it was the toxicity of associated pneumonia that was the killer.

A postscript is provided in Mr H J Howard's auctioneer's notice of a sale on 4th and 5th September 1919. The sale was held in the grounds of All Saints Hospital. Listed were 200 folding deck chairs, 30 new wicker bath chairs, 12 gramophones with a large quantity of records, books, games, puzzles and card tables. In addition to the usual hospital impedimenta of clothing and linen a wooden sectional building 100 feet long by 24 feet wide fitted with a stage and equipped as a cinema was also on offer. Clearly the troops' welfare needs had been more than adequately looked after.

5. THE RED CROSS AUXILIARY HOSPITALS

In August 1914 the War Office called on the British Red Cross Society nationally to provide hospitals to treat the war wounded. This fulfilled a provision in the Society's charter to render assistance to the government in time of war. In Sussex 44 war auxiliary hospitals would be provided by the Society. The distinguished visitors' lists in the local newspapers gave way to lists of names and units of British soldiers admitted to the Eastbourne War Hospitals.

9 Upperton Road 1917

In 1912 an Eastbourne entrepreneur, Mr Charles Jewell of Silverdale Road, who had made his fortune farming in Argentina persuaded a group of local businessmen to raise £2,000 to buy adjoining houses numbers 25 and 27 Upperton Road to be used as a British Soldiers and Sailors Home. The aims of the home were to assist disabled ex-servicemen back to health and train them in employable skills. This home was to become the first Red Cross auxiliary hospital in the town.

The lecture hall of the Upperton Congregational Church was also pressed into service as an annexe. Between them some 43 patients could be accommodated. The staff led by Sister McCartie, the matron of the home, included a deaconess, Sister Latimer, who had served as a district nurse. Other trained nurses and members of the Eastbourne Red Cross VADs assisted them The church formed a rota of ladies who helped with nursing and domestic duties. This hospital which opened October 1914 closed in June 1915 by which time it had became evident that the facilities were inadequate.

To meet the increasing demands a move was made to **No 9 Upperton Road** formerly St Celine's girls school which had gone into insolvency. In more recent memory this building housed The Maternity Home, latterly Health Authority offices and Ambulance Control Centre. Patients were accommodated in twin-bedded wards named after war heroes Cavell, Beatty, French, Jellicoe and Dorrien-Smith. An open air ward was added using a sectional wooden hut. The hospital opened with 40 beds which later increased to 70. During its period of service 1,400 cases were admitted. This was in addition to outpatients and Ministry of Pensions cases. In three and a half years only one patient was lost, Private George Cooke age 22 of the Lincolnshire Regiment who died on 11th November 1916 after a long illness. He is buried in Ocklynge Cemetery. The War Office prohibited the treatment of tuberculosis patients in the War Auxiliary Hospitals, but the Red Cross circumvented this by funding a TB spine case in the Upperton Hospital. Medical Officers gave their services and there were two paid nursing sisters. Volunteers carried out he rest of the work including domestic service. The hospital had a turnover of £12,367 in four years and the final surplus of £700 was distributed to local hospitals. The hospital opened in November 1915, continuing in service until December 1918.

With the severity of the fighting in France and the growing number of wounded needing treatment the War Office called for additional hospital facilities in 1915. Leases were secured or donated on a number of large properties in lower Meads. Wish Rocks in Blackwater Road; Kempston and opposite Urmston at the corner of Granville and Blackwater Roads,

Patients at Urmston Red Cross hospital

Redburn, Carlisle Road latterly known as Chelmsford Hall School. Fairfield Court, Carlisle Road and De Walden Court in Meads Road completed the group of hospitals in the town. During 1917 and 1918 each hospital managed to secure Council permission to have sectional wooden huts, for recreational purposes, erected in the grounds. This was usually followed by an increase in the hospital's bed capacity. The hospitals held voluntary fund raising efforts and some per capita government funding would have been received. Costings of four shillings per patient per day were the norm!

The War Office graded establishments according to the needs of the patients. The Red Cross auxiliary hospitals in Eastbourne came in category 1 able to treat severe cases which might need surgery, X-ray and massage facilities. In category 2 were convalescent camps such as the one in Summerdown Road. These would receive ambulant patients who had completed major care but would need a period of medically supervised convalescence. Such patients would have occupational therapy, massage, good food and recreational facilities. The third category were Command Depots where the men would have finished convalescence but would need a graded programme of restoration to A1 physical fitness before returning to active duty. The Cavalry Command Depot in Victoria Drive came within this category. There would be an interchange of patients between these facilities according to need. Patients from the Eastbourne Hospitals were also sent to convalescent homes at East Grinstead and Tunbridge Wells.

Patients and staff at Fairfield Court

Urmston, 55 Blackwater Road, was offered by Captain Morris in the second week of August 1914, and by 23rd September it was ready to receive patients. It had 65 beds and was run in conjunction with **Fairfield Court**, 26 Carlisle Road, which opened on 15th October 1915 with 75 beds finally increasing to 120. Mrs R Burke, wife of the Duke of Devonshire's agent, was the Commandant of BRCS Sussex 2 detachment, and was in charge of the two hospitals. In the first six months there were 573 admissions and 135 operations. The first convoy of wounded British soldiers arrived from the station in buses and taxis on 20th January 1915. Many of these men were suffering from frostbite, and some were taken to the Wish Rocks Hospital. After a Belgian soldier Andre van den Bosch died on 10th March 1915, his funeral procession to Ocklynge Cemetery was led by the band of the Loyal North Lancashire Regiment. Another soldier Private William Brown age 21 of the RAMC died from meningitis on 25th April 1915. Later in June, Private Weedon Douglas Bellman, a local Territorial soldier with the London Cyclists, died of wounds received at La Basse he was subsequently buried in Ocklynge. In June 1916 one of the Urmston nurses Miss C M Hodges, died from septicaemia after caring for sick soldiers. The band of the 13th Hussars led the funeral procession to Ocklynge Cemetery where buglers sounded the last post. The firing party was provided by soldiers from the Cavalry Command Depot, Victoria Drive. In June 1917 Private Harry Gee aged 23 from the 33rd Battalion Australian Infantry died from a haemorrhage whilst under anaesethic. He had been admitted to Fairfield Court direct from France with bullet wound in the throat.

Wish Rocks, 47 Blackwater Road, lent by Mr H H Simmonds of Hailsham as a hospital received its first convoy of Belgian wounded on 14th October 1914. Part of the convoy of wounded were sent to the Leaf Hospital in Marine Road. The Wish Rocks hospital was staffed by BRCS Sussex 12 detachment under the command of Lady Wilson. During its use as a hospital 375 patients were treated there. Accident cases often were taken to the nearest hospital. A car smash at the corner of Grange Road and Blackwater Roads in June 1915 resulted in a party of officers and their ladies being admitted for treatment. The building was found to be impractical to operate so a move was made to **De Walden Court**, Meads Road, opened in December 1915 with 90 beds. The house was made available by the London Counties and Westminster Bank.

Red Cross men and Ambulances await a hospital train

Kempston, 3 Granville Road, opened on 15th March 1915 by Mrs Davies Gilbert with Miss Sulman as Commandant and Miss Tweed as Matron. It was staffed by BRCS Sussex 100 detachment, which also supplied staff to the Soldiers and Sailors Home in Upperton Road. It had 38 beds mostly six to a ward. There were four trained nurses, 40 VADs, 12 cooks, pantry maids and domestics.. The most serious cases were in downstairs rooms. Two RAMC men were used to help with heavy lifting. Command Medical specialists paid regular visits to the hospital and

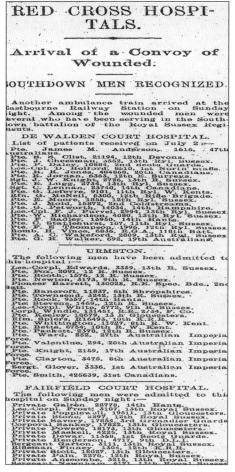

RED CROSS HOSPITALS.

Arrival of a Convoy of Wounded.

SOUTHDOWN MEN RECOGNIZED.

Another ambulance train arrived at the Eastbourne Railway Station on Sunday night. Among the wounded men were several who have been serving in the Southdown battalion of the Royal Sussex Regiments.

DE WALDEN COURT HOSPITAL.
List of patients received on July 2 :—
Australians.
Pte. James M. Anderson, 1616. 47th
Pte. S. R. Cliat, 21194, 12th Devons.
Pte. J. Cheesman, 4552, 13th Ryl. Sussex.
Pte. F. Daley, 1086, 2nd Scots Guards.
Lce-Cpl. D. Halford, 810, 1st North Staffs.
Pte. R. R. Jones, 404860, 20th Canadians.
Pte. H. Jordian, 6363, 12th R. Surreys.
Sgt. J. W. Knight, 2726, 13th R. Sussex.
Pte. E. Legg, 3734, 13th Ryl. Sussex.
Sgt. L. Lennan, 23740, 14th Canadians.
Pte. G. Lefevre, 9101, 11th Ryl. W. Kents.
Rfn. G. McNeill, 6906, 12th Rifle Brigade.
Pte. E. Moore, 1855, 12th Ryl. Sussex.
Pte. J. Mold, 13873, 2nd Coldstreams.
Pte. G. Petworth, 14034, 14th Hampshire.
Lce-Cpl. F. J. Purcel, 2994, 13th Ryl. Sussex
Pte. W. Richardson, 4080, 13th Ryl. Sussex.
Pte. F. Sadler, 13950, 14th Hants.
Pte. C. Stanlehurst, 107, 11th Ryl. Sussex.
Pte. F. E. Thompson, 996, 12th Ryl. Sussex.
Bomb. A. Wakeford, 2809, 13th Ryl. Sussex
Pte. G. H. Walker, 692, 19th Australians.

URMSTON.
The following men have been admitted to this hospital :—
Corpl. Edwards, 3339, 13th R. Sussex.
Pte. Fox, 3091, 13 R. Sussex.
Pte. Booth, 1576, 12 R. Sussex.
Pte. Newton, 31751, 9th R. Sussex.
Pioneer Barrett, 150028, R.E. Spec. Bde., 2nd
Batt.
Pte. Bancroft, 11837, 6th Shropshires.
Pte. Gowbssard, 3242, 13th R. Sussex.
Pte. Rook, 9357, 14th Hants.
Ptel Stevens, 1469, 12th R. Sussex.
Lce-Corpl. White, 6772, 9th R. Sussex.
Corpl Windle, 1514513, R.E. 2/34, F. Co.
Pte. Keeley, 18679, 13 R. Gloucesters.
Rfm Spiers, R14649, 10th K. R. R.
Pte. Whittington, 11727, 8th R. W. Kent.
Pte. Packktat, 2378, 12th R. Sussex.
Pte. Ward, 252, 27th Australian Imperial
Force.
Pte. Valentine, 294, 20th Australian Imperial
Force.
Pte. Knight, 2159, 17th Australian Imperial
Force.
Pte. Clayton, 3475, 8th Australian Imperial
Force.
Sergt. Glover, 3436, 1st Australian Imperial
Force.
Pte. Smith, 425639, 31st Canadians.

FAIRFIELD COURT HOSPITAL.
The following men were admitted to this hospital on Sunday night :—
Private Galpin, 22778, 14th Hants.
Lce-Corpl. Frost, 3107, 13th Royal Sussex.
Private Popplewell, 19611, 13th Gloucesters.
Private Stone, 2297, 12th Royal Sussex.
Private Savory, 1785, 2nd Grenadier Guards
Corporal Sankey, 17822, 13th Gloucesters.
Private Powers, 18172, 13th Royal Sussex.
Private Maskell, 4225, 13th Royal Sussex.
Private Dewar, 11359, 1st Scots Guards.
Private Henderson, 4717, 9th D.L.I.
Sergeant Garton, 3111, 13th Royal Sussex.
Rifleman Finney, 1304, 12th K.R.R.
Private Stott, 18027, 13th Gloucesters.
Private Pain, 2270, 12th Royal Sussex.
Private Anscombe, 3216, 13th Royal Sussex.
Sergeant Newnham, 4171, 13th Royal Sussex.

Admission list June 1916

would use the fully equipped operating theatre. Manor Hall was used as an annexe for three months closing in December 1915. In December 1916 Gunner Walter Rourke, Warwickshire RFA, died soon after admission to Kempston from a Dover Ambulance train. In early June 1916 an aeroplane pilot, Lieutenant L C Keble injured after crashing was taken to Kempston where he recovered. Six patients of Kempston who died are commemorated on a memorial in St Peter's and St Saviours Church, South Street.

Redburn, 71 Carlisle Road, opened with 32 beds on 1st April 1916. In the first half year it treated 100 cases with costs of £1,432. It was the last of the hospitals to close at the end of the war. Over 500 cases were thought to have been dealt with in in two and half years. One of the VAD nurses at Redburn was a Miss L D Harington who became the mother of Mr D G Stevens the last headmaster of Chelmsford Hall. The school which occupied Redburn from January 1920 was named after its patron, Lord Chelmsford Viceroy of India 1916-1921. Mr Stevens' father Colonel L C Stevens, first headmaster of the school, had been a member of the Eastbourne battery of the 2nd Home Counties RFA and ADC to Lord Chelmsford.

By the end of the war in 1918, De Walden Court had treated 3,000 cases, Urmston 2,923 and Fairfield Court with Kempston 2,569. Closure of the auxiliary hospitals followed quickly, and by the end of December 1918 all were shut. Auction sales of surplus equipment followed early in 1919. The sale at De Walden Court conducted by Oakden's auctioneers realised £318 but the Solus X-ray machine failed to find a buyer. Mr Barratt Terry, auctioneer advertised a revolving summerhouse as part of the Redburn effects. Suggestions that De Walden Court might become a Soldiers' and Sailors' Home, and Fairfield Court could possibly be a War Memorial Art Gallery, never came to fruition.

In the early days patients would be brought to Eastbourne Station by trains with ordinary coaches for sitting cases and parcel vans for those on stretchers. In November 1915 a new ambulance train constructed at the Lancing works of the London, Brighton and South Coast Railway was exhibited at platform one at Eastbourne station, this attracting over 2,000 visitors. It was composed of 16 eight wheeled bogie coaches, comprising four ward cars with 120 beds, two kitchen cars, one pharmacy car with treatment room equipped with an urn and sterilizer, should operations be needed. An office, stores and separate linen store were provided. Five sitting case cars for 320 patients including one for 64 infectious disease cases. The infectious disease car had perforated plywood seats to avoid cross infection through contaminated upholstery. Two kitchen cars with army ranges could produce 50 gallons of hot water per hour from two 150 gallon roof water storage tanks. Accommodation for 28 staff was provided in self heating cars. With two brake vans a further 18 infectious cases could be taken. The complete train was 930 feet long and weighed 420 tons.

Hospital trains would usually arrive at Eastbourne from Dover but on occasion from as far away as Devonport. At the station the trains would be met and unloaded by Red Cross volunteers, the patients being transported to hospitals by bus, taxi and private cars with up to 50 cars being used at a time. The frequency of the train arrivals mirrored the activity on the battlefields, even without a major action a steady flow of casualties resulted from trench warfare, sniping, grenade attacks, shellfire, gassing and accidents. A monthly arrival was the norm but a weekly arrival followed periods of intense fighting. In September 1916 in the final days of the battle of the Somme a train brought 189 cases, 100 on stretchers, the rest walking wounded. It was reported that a large number of Red Cross volunteers helped. By the time of the last great German spring offensive in 1918 arrivals were received in a practiced way. On 29th March, 12 ambulances and three buses were used for 60 cot and 96 stretcher cases. Again in April, 68 cases were cleared from the station in 40 minutes by a team of 88 Red Cross men. The ambulances were those donated by Caffyn's and Lovely's Garages, together with others from Clovelly-Kepplestone School. Army ambulances from the Central Military Hospital and the Canadian Hospital at All Saints were also used. About half the number of vehicles used were sent by road from the Brighton Red Cross detachment. By today's standards the vehicles were quite primitive being unheated and having canvas bodies on commercial springing. Racks held four stretchers, with the back of the ambulance being closed with a canvas roll down sheet.

Other Establishments

Fernbrook 1 Hartington Place had been a large villa type residence in private occupation in 1914. In 1917 it was taken over by a Roman Catholic order for use as a convalescent hospital for officers. It continued to give service in this way until 1919. In 1921 Pike's Blue Book recorded it as being a Medical and Surgical Nursing Home, the forerunner of the Esperance Private Hospital. **Staveley Court** in Staveley Road operated as a convalescent home for officers with 20 beds. It received its patients from the Central Officers Hospital, Chichester Terrace, Brighton. At Hailsham, Dr T S Taylor offered the use of his house at **39 North Street** for use as a hospital. This unit opened in January 1915 with wounded Belgian soldiers as its first patients. The hospital had 21 beds receiving patients from Urmston. The medical supervision was provided by the Central Military Hospital.

Pevensey Bay Red Cross Convalescent home was a joint venture by the Sussex and Marylebone Red Cross Divisions, not for war wounded but a rehabilitation centre for Red Cross workers exhausted by their efforts in the London auxiliary hospitals. Mrs Val Prinseps' agent applied to the Eastbourne Rural District Council in March 1917 for permission to erect

Pevensey Red Cross volunteers

five wood and iron bungalows at Pevensey Bay. Despite support from the Honorary Secretary of the Society, the Clerk to the Rural Council pointed out that the buildings did not comply with the regulations and would not be suitable for human habitation. Finally temporary permission was given for a period terminating six months after the end of the war. In July of that year a further application had to be made to vary the consent to allow the construction to be in brick and concrete as there was a war time shortage of wood. The Sanitary Inspector was given delegated powers to act. The buildings materialized in the end and are recorded in J A Hammerton's "Great War, I Was There" 1938. The opening of the first bungalow took place in June 1917, the funds for which had been given together with the land by Mrs Val Prinseps. The dwellings were later described as ex-army huts and named "The Boxes". These Hutments stood in front of the building line and this allowed their replacement by Anthony Prinseps' property, the "Pink House", built in 1935 in "The French Riviera Style" and known latterly as "Courtlands".

6. SUMMERDOWN AND THE BLUE BOYS

By 1914 Pashley Road had been delineated with just two houses being completed. The area to the south known as Summerdown together with Motcombe Laines and its decaying farm buildings amounted to about 50

The main camp road looking towards Summerdown Road

acres of land below the scarp of the Downs on the west of the town. By the Duke of Devonshire's benevolence it had been a popular venue for the Sussex Agricultural Show in previous years. Although situated on the edge of Old Town it was close to the workhouse in Church Street and commended itself to the military authorities who were seeking to establish a training centre for the Royal Army Medical Corps in Old Town.

Kitchener's volunteers had been drafted into the RAMC and some had been housed in billets in the town whilst others were under canvas at Cow Gap. The bad weather during the Autumn of 1914 and the exposed position of Cow Gap lent a sense of urgency to the provision of better accommodation for these men. Local building firms were contracted to construct wooden huts on the Summerdown site under the supervision of Mr Roland Burke, the Duke's agent, who acted as clerk of works for the Chief Royal Engineer of Eastern Command.

The camp lines looking to East Dean Road

In October plans were being implemented and by December arrangements were in hand to extend the electricity cables to provide sufficient current to light 500 lamps, the transformer and 400 yards of cable from Church Street, costing a total of £44. By January 1915 five rows of wooden huts had been built on brick bases, identified in lines lettered A to E. Each hut measured 60 by 15 feet with sufficient room to accommodate 30 men. Toilets, showers, bathrooms, drying and mess rooms were provided. At the entrance to the camp in Summerdown Road a brick built Guardroom with detention cells was located. Army issue stoves were used for heating. Pathways were of ash or chalk but in wet weather muddy conditions prevailed. Accommodation had been provided for 3,500 men although some tents remained in use. The roads and pathways totalled five miles whilst there were two miles each of underground water pipes and drains. A new sewer had to be laid in Summerdown Road as far as what is now Old Camp Road, the council allowing abutting properties to be connected. A Royal Engineers' workshop was on site and all stores were provided by the Army Service Corps. The construction work on the camp and its roads led to an excessive demand for chalk which was obtained from the Duke of Devonshire's pit in East Dean Road. The pit now a housing development, Ridgelands Close, was opposite the Sanatorium, latterly Downside Hospital, The traffic led to the road breaking up and repairs being paid for by the War Office.

The first convalescents arrived in April 1915, and by September the run down of RAMC trainees was almost complete and convalescent "Blue Boys" were taking up the now vacated accommodation. Since the Crimean War soldiers recovering from wounds or sickness had worn distinctive clothing. This made recognition easier for Military Police controlling curfews, which for Summerdown was 9.00 pm. A soldier in a Cambridge blue jacket with white reveres, matching trousers, white shirt and red tie would instantly be recognised by the inhabitants of Eastbourne as a recovering soldier from Summerdown Camp. The mass of casualties, in hospitals and convalescent units was spread throughout the United Kingdom. The blue uniform would secure sympathetic consideration from the civilian population of the garrison towns where the military hospitals were located.

Summerdown being a category 2 establishment in addition to providing basic medical treatment, would offer rehabilitation, occupational therapy, massage (physiotherapy), good food, sporting, cultural, social and entertainment facilities. The residents warmed to the camp and its occupants and nothing was too much trouble to help the men recuperate. The men for their part reciprocated and entered fully into the life of the town. Despite the ever-changing population of the camp it boasted a fine band which in addition to playing at the camp for an hour each morning would, in the summer, give concerts at the Royal Parade Bandstand and on the Pier. From 18th September 1915 until 1920 "The Summerdown Journal" was printed fortnightly costing one penny per issue. Issue Number 1 gave an account of the Commanding Officer formerly Major and latterly Colonel, Bostock who had previously been in charge of a convalescent camp in France. Colonel Bostock except for a short absence in France remained in charge of the camp for most of its life, the last CO being Colonel E P Powell.

A sleeping hut

The Journal also contained a variety of reports including 200 missing blankets, the replacement of male cooks by members of the Women's Auxiliary Army Corps (WAAC) and the availability of gardening tuition. This was organised by a local resident, Miss Winifrid Pattison, and a team of ladies. The Chaplain wrote that services would soon be held in a purpose built chapel instead of the YMCA tent, and that the Bishop of Lewes would hold a Confirmation Service. Local residents donated an organ, carpets and altar frontals. Later issues gave news of the" Kamp Komedey Knuts Koncert" (KKKK) Party, which in addition to in-house entertainment would tour the other hospitals in the town. Six-a-side football matches were organised and sporting fixtures would be arranged with men from Polegate Airship Station and the Flying Training School at St Anthony's Hill aerodrome. Two YMCA workers arrived from Cambridge to start welfare work in a marquee, which was soon replaced by a large hut. About the same time a camp post office was opened.

Pay parade in front of the YMCA canteen

The Tivoli Cinema lent equipment and films for a fortnightly Sunday cinema show. The Council had refused to allow Sunday cinema opening in the town. On 24th February 1916 a new concert hall given by Mr Roland Burke was opened. It was the largest single building on the site measuring 180 by 30 feet of corrugated iron lined with matchboarding and had a raked floor. The building could seat 1,500 men, which was half the camp at one sitting. It was heated with slow combustion stoves and forced air ventilation was installed. The exit doors were fitted with panic bars. The stage was 45 feet wide by 20 feet deep. The proscenium was emblazoned with G R and the flags of the Allies. A sunken orchestra pit completed the theatre arrangements. Local firms including Bainbridge's carried out electrical work with Plummer's supplying the stage and other curtains. Outside the clock tower housed a clock given by Bruford's. When not in use for entertainment the building doubled as a gymnasium.

The Empire club

Outside activities continued, with one of the most popular being the coach and motor drives usually ending with a tea. Chapman's coach proprietors provided some of the vehicles. The Eastbourne Corporation Bus Department provided many of the coaches charging one shilling per mile and using voluntary drivers. Many residents lent private cars and paid for teas during the trip. An arts and crafts competition produced over 100 entries. A sea-angling contest took place on the Pier. During the winter it was cold enough to skate on the Hampden Park pond. A summer gymkhana was held at Compton Place in aid of the Red Cross Hospitals and was attended by men and the band from Summerdown. Lady French, wife of the C-in-C, presented the prizes.

Men arriving at Eastbourne railway station for Summerdown would travel free on the Old Town Bus to the Tally Ho terminus. The Corporation reclaiming the one penny fare from the War Office. This gives an index of activity with 11,567 penny fare passes issued between

1st April and 27th November 1915. In March 1916 it was noted that 1,000 patients were in the camp. By the first anniversary 20,000 had been treated. Of the 8,012 discharged in a six-month period, 91% were fit to return to active service. Pictures of contingents being marched down Church Street, headed by the band, en route for the station, France and the infamous base camp at Etaples, demonstrate the men's return to fitness.

Not all the convalescents returned to service. In January 1915 Private George Griffiths of the 73rd Field Ambulance RAMC who had suffered "Gastric Trouble" was found dead in bed. Private Archibald Davies, 1st Dorsetshire Regiment, died in June 1915, whilst recovering from being gassed in France. Private Harry G---, Machine Gun Corps, a former dentist, died in January 1919 from a septic abscess. He had been on fatigue duty in the Dispensary in the Central Military Hospital and was a known drug addict. Puncture marks were seen on his body after death. He had previously been at Summerdown for a year. The bandsmen of Summerdown were often called on to play at military funerals at Ocklynge for those who died at the town's hospitals or had been brought home to Eastbourne after succumbing at hospitals elsewhere in England. Summerdown being an RAMC establishment would not have had an armoury or weapons. Firing parties for funerals were provided by the men at the Command Depot in Victoria Drive or by Canadians from the Seaford Camps, or by other available units in the town.

The Almeric Paget Military Massage Corps

The practice of massage and remedial gymnastics as a supplement to medical treatment of patients had existed since the late nineteenth century. Some masseuses had little or no formal training whilst others had undergone formal courses and belonged to professional bodies. The Director of Army Medical Services, Sir Alfred Keogh, sought to speed the treatment and recovery of sick and wounded soldiers. In order to do this he set up four large convalescent camps at Blackpool, Epsom, Dartford and Summerdown at Eastbourne. These camps freed hospital beds and at the same time offered the most advanced physiotherapy treatments given by properly trained masseuses. Training demanded two years at a Physical Training College or certification from the Incorporated Society of Trained Masseuses or a six-month practical training course.

Sir Alfred Keogh enlisted the aid of Mrs Almeric Paget, wife of the Member of Parliament for Cambridge, in this project. Mrs Pauline Payne

Mrs Almeric Paget and the Massage Corps

Almeric Paget, daughter of George C Whitney, former Secretary of the United States Navy, was a wealthy American who had married into the aristocratic Anglesey family. Within a few weeks of the outbreak of the war the services of 50 certificated masseuses were sought for the first centre at the Paget's London home, 39 Berkeley Street where over 150 treatments were given daily. The centre was equipped and maintained by the Pagets. The Honorary Secretary was Miss Eleanor Essex French, daughter of Sir John French Commander of the British Expeditionary Force in France. Dr Florence Barrie Lambert was the Honorary Medical

Officer. With such patronage, success was assured and all three ladies were frequent visitors to Summerdown.

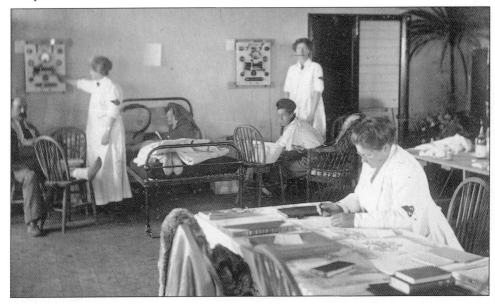

Treatments in the massage room

The Corps uniform consisted of a dark blue ankle length skirt, a jacket with a woven badge, white shirt, dark blue tie and dark felt hat. For duty, a white overall and cap with the badge was provided. The treatments given included massage, physical exercises, muscle extension, heat, vibratory, electrical and chemical solutions. Thirty-two masseuses each treated up to 25 patients a day. Each masseuse would attend to four patients at a time. Cases of trench foot received sinusoidal baths, massage and foot exercises. Septic wounds received galvanic current, the bacteria going to the positive pole. Functional paralysis from shell shock required strong Faradism and Swedish exercises. Daily exercises would be given to groups of men recovering from the effects of gassing. The staff changed dressings and it is recorded that a treatment of Sciatica included painting of the nerve with fuming hydrochloric acid! The Massage Institute at Summerdown was housed in a large wooden building, the main block being 120 by 30 feet with two additional wings of 30 by 30 feet. There was also a further Electrotherapy building measuring 85 by 25 feet containing cubicles. To complete the complex there were separate battery and store rooms.

The Angel of Summerdown

Mrs Almeric Paget has been described as a philanthropist and this she was to the full. Her kindness to the Blue Boys endeared her to the men and did much to speed their recovery. When she came to visit the camp she took up residence at Compton Place. Any need of the camp brought to her notice received a ready response. She provided the instruments for the band, and a bell for the chapel. At Christmas 1915 she paid for all those well enough to go the pantomime at the Theatre Royal, Brighton. The men went in batches by coach. Those going to the afternoon performance were entertained to tea at the Royal Crescent Hotel. Those going to the evening show went to a supper beforehand.

Mrs Paget impersonated by Kamp Komedy artist

On one of her visits in early 1916 she was accompanied by her brother-in- law's wife, Lady Victor Paget, who would have been better known as Miss Olive May, the actress. Mrs Paget made her last visit to Compton Place and Summerdown in September 1916 shortly afterwards on 22nd November she died suddenly at the early age of 41. Mrs Paget had not enjoyed good health for a number of years and suffered a fatal heart attack at Esher in Surrey. The funeral took place at Hertingfordbury near Hertford. The Blue Boys had lost their Lady

Bountiful, and the camp band travelled to Hertford to lead the funeral cortège. Her will disclosed an estate of £200,000, a vast sum in those far off days. Her memory lived in on the work of the Massage Corps which bore her name. After Mrs Paget's death her husband, Mr Almeric Paget, MP, from 1918 Lord Queenborough, continued to support the Massage Corps. At the Armistice the corps was 2,000 strong, and in 1919 became known as the Military Massage Service with nearly 3,400 members who had served during the war.

The recreation room

Distinguished visitors came to the camp, the list being headed by King George V and Queen Mary who honoured the camp by visiting on 3rd May 1916. The wife of the Prime Minister, Mrs David Lloyd George, visited the camp in October 1918. From time to time, high ranking officers visited on behalf of HM the King to present decorations for distinguished conduct in the field. The public took up the opportunity to view the camp on an open day held in April 1916 when 2,000 local people visited Summerdown.

Whilst the men were in Summerdown those from the United Kingdom could receive visits from their families. For the private soldier on pay of one shilling a day this would be difficult as there was no camp accommodation for conjugal visits. Miss Alston of Arklow House, 51, Summerdown Road arranged for a hostel to be set up for the wives and children of Summerdown men to use during visits to the town. The Empire Hostel was opened in September 1915 at 51, Upperton Gardens. Adults paid ten shillings per week, accompanying children paid just one shilling. In the first nine months it was reported that 200 guests had been accommodated. A second house next door was leased and by the time the Empire Hostel closed in March 1919 it had accommodated 1,500 guests and the weekly charge had increased to fourteen shillings. A final surplus of £159 was donated to Camp amenity funds.

Gymnasium/Theatre with Brufords clock tower

The need for Summerdown's existence fortunately came to end in January 1920 when it was the last wartime establishment in Eastbourne to close. The final outside concert given by the KKKK was on 27th January in the Victoria Hall, Hailsham, in aid of the United Friendly

Societies. The members of Queen Mary's Auxiliary Army Corps were given a farewell dinner and concert on 11th December 1919. Ceremonial photographs were taken of the RAMC staff, the Massage Corps, and the few remaining patients dressed not in "Blues" but unusually in khaki with their unit badges displayed. Farewell concerts were held with the title "Hello Civvies" on 17th February 1920.

Auctioneers, Edgar Horn were charged with the disposal of the Camp buildings and equipment. The market for war surplus buildings and material had been saturated locally and nationally. So great was the number of buildings and quantity of equipment to be disposed of that six sale days over a period 13 months were required to clear the site. The first sale took place on 27th January 1921 with the final sale taking place on 18th February 1922, and this last sale realising £2,562.

Closedown photograph of staff and patients

Some extracted highlights of the auctioneer's particulars illustrate the complexity of the establishment and provide clues to the type and size of the structures. The auctioneers described the huts as being suitable for use as bungalows, residences, public halls, mission halls, garages, workshops and poultry buildings. In all 252 buildings ranging from sleeping huts measuring 60 by 20 feet to the 145 feet long gymnasium complete with clock tower. Four railway carriages were also available.

The sale notices also identified the uses the buildings had been put to, for example, dental clinic, regimental institute, skittle alley, chapel, orderly room and officer's mess. The equipment ranged from 1,066 pillows, 691 iron bedsteads, 583 tables, 161 candlesticks, 89 shaving bowls, 10 stomach warmers, 694 window blinds, 13 slop carts, 554 shelf brackets and 271 taps.

The fate of two of the buildings is known, the wooden guard room was sold for £63. It was transported to the Eastbourne Downs Golf Club where it did duty as an equipment store close to the eleventh tee. It was finally pulled down in 1972. The Theatre Gymnasium building was purchased for use as a sports pavilion. The directors of the London Metropolitan Railway had given its staff association the sum of £5,000 to commemorate those lost in the war. The Theatre Gymnasium was secured for the sum of £250, dismantled and transported to the Forty Lane, Wembley Park, sports ground where it remained for a few short years as the Remembrance Hall until it became a total loss through fire in 1929.

Sleeping huts were sold for £38, the Regimental Institute made £150 and the Massage Institute fetched £145. Post war private housing development soon covered the area. With the naming of Old Camp Road the memory of Summerdown Camp and the Blue Boys was perpetuated. In all probability the line taken by the main camp road had been decided before the war when the Summerdown estate was planned. So the road foundations were installed at the War Office's expense. Another legacy of the camp is the photographic record which consists mainly of postcards, these were produced in variety and in great quantities. With an ever changing camp population purchasing the cards, there was little commercial reason for producing new pictures after the end of 1915. Tighter censorship restricted photography so that there is little pictorial record of the camp later in the war.

64

Plan of Summerdown Camp showing main hutted areas (not to scale)

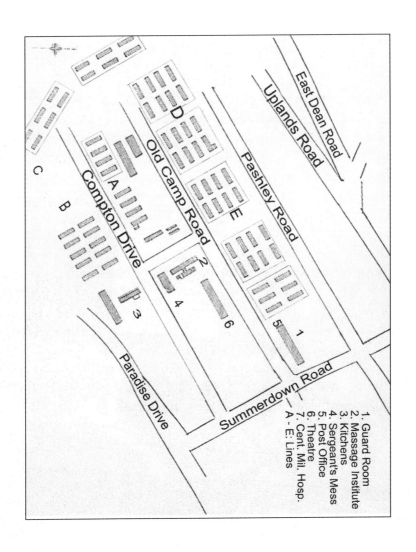

1. Guard Room
2. Massage Institute
3. Kitchens
4. Sergeant's Mess
5. Post Office
6. Theatre
7. Cent. Mil. Hosp.
A - E: Lines

7. THE CAVALRY COMMAND DEPOT

Command Depots were created to bring men up to a standard of physical fitness for return to front line duty after convalescence from injury or sickness. Command Depots were category 3 establishments after main hospitals and Convalescent camps. Early in 1916 the War Office sought to establish a Cavalry Command Depot in Eastbourne. A suitable site presented itself at the edge of the then built-up area in Old Town on the west side of Victoria Drive near to the junction with Green Street. Today the area is easily recognisable as the land behind the Merry Fiddler, until recently, the Drive Hotel. The site is bounded by Beechy Avenue to the north and Victoria Gardens to the south.

Site of Cavalry Command depot 1929 with hutment homes for heroes

The six acre parcel of land had until 1914 been in the ownership of the Duke of Devonshire. In that year the Eastbourne Corporation had decided to take powers under the Housing of the Working Classes Acts (1890) to build council housing. To this end plots of land had been identified at the Archery and in Victoria Drive. The Victoria Drive plot being the subject of the requisition order for the Command Depot. It is ironic that the Hutments erected for the army on this site lasted for ten years after the Armistice as temporary housing. The conditions were a far cry from those envisaged in the popular slogan of the returning soldiers "Homes Fit For Heroes".

In March 1916 the Corporation had agreed to the extension of electricity cables to supply the new depot's power requirement of 200 light bulbs. The cable costing £172 would be run the length of Eldon Road. Approval in March for a new five-inch water main was obtained. Mr Roland Burke the former agent of the Duke of Devonshire now in uniform as the District Officer Royal Engineers would supervise the construction of the depot. This would consist of some brick buildings but the majority would be wooden Hutments constructed of matchboarding covered with canvas. A total of 110 huts of various sizes were erected in rows 30 feet apart and arranged in lines lettered A to G. The OS map 1/1250 of 1925 gives a clear indication of the layout although by this time some 64 huts out of the original 115 remained on site. The remainder having been sold or removed to allow the building of Victoria Gardens and Beechy Avenue.

The Depot, Commanded by Colonel Follett, opened in June 1916 and it was planned to accommodate 2,000 men. From the recorded size and number of the huts on site 2,000 men would have had to be accommodated in three tiered bunks. After the war when the huts were used as housing a maximum of 600 persons accommodated was reached in 1923. In 1916 there were 600 South African troops undergoing recuperative training. Many of these would have come from the South

African Red Cross Hospital in Richmond Park, London. The men of the South African Brigade were known as "Springboks". They were probably survivors of a costly attack at Delville Wood on the Somme in July 1916. In a week's fighting their numbers were reduced from 3,000 to 800 men. On arrival a man would be interviewed and assessed by a Medical Board for fitness and suitability for the various types of training. The men were organised into 4 squadrons by merit of fitness, and could be identified by coloured tabs on their epaulets. Red signified the most able followed by green, blue and yellow, the latter for the least able. The gymnasium was supervised by a medical officer. It was equipped with rowing machines fitted with sliding seats, pulley developers, grip rollers and grip bars. Treadles, Indian clubs and throwing bags containing seven pounds of gravel complemented the more conventional equipment such as vaulting horses, boxes and climbing ropes. The red badge group would be ready to return to front line duty within seven to ten days. The second green group would be deemed fit for bayonet practice, the third blue group would engage in assault courses whilst the new arrivals, yellow tabs, would do balancing on and gymnastics with tree trunks. Each man's progress would be reviewed by the medical officer at 14 day intervals.

The depot band was composed of competent young able musicians of the 13th Hussars but suffered continual change. As soon as the bandsmen reached 18 years of age they were drafted to France. The band played at public functions as well as in camp and they occupied the Parade Bandstand for a programme of music on Bastille Day in 1917. A less pleasurable duty would be at Ocklynge Cemetery where they would often be called on to sound the Last Post at some of the 130 military funerals whilst their comrades would provide the firing parties. The Camp boasted a concert party known as the Cavalry Command Cripples Concert Party again like their counterparts at Summerdown they would entertain not only the depot men but those in the local hospitals. One of the performers caught the attention of the local papers a Sergeant George Robey, a member of the transport section. He was an established music hall performer who later attained popularity in the inter-war years in variety theatres and on radio. A rough and ready fire alarm signal in the camp consisted of an iron bar run along boundary metal railings. The army atmosphere was confirmed by the unofficial Depot Motto picked out in white stones "Hors de Combat" best seen, it was reported from the air. An Open Day arranged in August 1917 attracted 3,000 visitors. Sport formed an important part of the treatment. Tournaments were organised between the colour groups and other service units in the town with the Old Town Recreation ground being reserved for football matches two days per week. Cricket, tennis and fencing also featured on the programme. Gardening was another depot pursuit.

By September 1917 the activity at the depot slackened and the numbers began to run down. The opportunity was taken to renovate some of the huts and the depot name changed to Officers' Command Depot. The officers would be accommodated in billets and the other ranks in the depot. Before the new arrangements could be fully implemented the war ended and by December 1918 the depot was closed.

An auction sale was arranged for 21st January 1919 for the contents and equipment under the hammer of R Barratt Terry. The items listed included office furniture, typewriters, 600 novels (well kept), two nearly new bacon slicers, two potato cleaning machines of 56 pound capacity and a palm tree 10 feet tall and of 30 feet spread. Rain deterred buyers on the first day of the two-day sale. A railway coach fitted out as a post office made £27, typewriters went for £22 each, a safe £35, the palm tree £15. A wide variety of surplus gardening equipment, hand tools, mowers, rollers, sprayers and 2,000 sturdy wallflower plants ready for bedding out were available.

A grand piano made £45, a boxing ring failed to sell and was given to Summerdown Camp. Rumours that officers would share the proceeds were quickly dispelled, the income would be returned to the government.

A further sale was planned for July 1919 offering two large dining halls 130 feet by 30 feet, a drill hall 100 feet by 40 feet, a cookhouse, skittle alley and a coal enclosure. About 100 sectional wooden buildings with sash windows and doors, 11 brick buildings 60 feet by 15 feet, various furnaces, boilers, tanks, cisterns and plumbing sundries. In May the Government Surplus Disposals Board released 40 of the huts for sale. The remainder was purchased by the Council and at the same time the site was returned to them.

Homes Fit for Heroes

Two months after the Officers Command Depot closed in January 1919 the Council asked the Local Government Board to clear the site as a matter of urgency. In March questions were put to the Council to consider the huts as temporary housing. Events moved quickly, the Duke of Devonshire offered to sell the Council the site of the Depot and 90 acres of adjoining land in April. At the end of May 1919 it was announced that the Command Depot huts were to be divided in two and used for housing, 226 applications having been made by prospective tenants.

One far seeing councillor expressed the hope that if the huts were to be used for housing that inside lavatories should be installed. This hope proved to be forlorn. Initially 15 families were housed, with another four huts becoming available being each week, it was hoped that by June 1919 80 families would have homes. The cost to the Council of each hut converted was £45 and the total cost of the scheme was £5,086. The YMCA asked about the fate of their hut hoping that it could be used as a Red Triangle club, but this was not to be.

A further 38 buildings had been purchased including the dining rooms main buildings at the entrance, brick latrines and ablution blocks at a cost of £8,296. Mr R D Knapp's application to use a hut at the entrance to the site as a temporary shop was approved. Mr Knapp's "Bungalow Stores" provided a valuable service for the hut dwellers and the homes being built in the area until the business was transferred in 1927 to a shop in the newly built Albert Parade. A request from the Rev W MacFadyn Scott for a hut to use as a mission hall for the Upperton Congregational Church was agreed and a large building on the north east side of the entrance was allocated for this purpose. The church abandoned its original intention to have a permanent church in the area following the opening of Victoria Drive Baptist Church in 1927.

Guardroom doing duty as Bungalow Stores (Mr A Knapp)

By November 1919 the Command Depot huts were described as a wooden town known generally as the "Hutments". These huts would be for the temporary easement of the housing crisis, whilst new Council houses were planned and built. It would not be until 1929 that the occupancy of the huts ceased. The pressure for better living accommodation had existed well before the war started in 1914, often three generations of a family would share a small working class property.

Wartime controls had stabilised rents at almost pre-war levels. Returns to landlords from investment property were poor, a disincentive to build and invest. For almost four years no new houses had been built and expectations of the returning servicemen had fuelled a huge demand for homes.

Rows of huts flank muddy paths

Mr F W Allcock acted as Clerk of Works for the building alterations being made to the huts. In addition he was appointed custodian of the site. Rents were five shillings per week for three to six persons having two, three or four rooms those having eight or nine rooms would pay six shillings and six pence. Two, three or four families would share the bigger huts. Monday was the rent collection day and no arrears were allowed to accrue. Mr Allcock acted as a "Mayor" of the township and settled disputes and also supervised the "Hutments "fire brigade. This consisted of a hose cart with 1,500 feet of hose and chemical extinguishers, all surplus depot equipment. Six residents were enrolled as temporary firemen. Mr Allcock had a site office in a Hut at the entrance to the depot that was equipped with a telephone for emergency purposes. The name of the depot became fixed in memory as "The Hutments" appearing as part of the postal address with the hut row and number. It also featured in the electoral roll and in street directories.

By 1920 there were 398 adults and 223 children in the Hutments. Each morning a school bus left at 8.40 am. Allotments and streetlights were part of the few amenities provided. The rents included an allowance for electricity at one 40 watt bulb per room, but it was soon found that this was financially unsound for the Council as many tenants had fitted stronger bulbs. One resident interviewed in 1998 recalled the conditions of life in the Hutments including the electricity curfew at 9.30 pm. One ex- soldier made a contemporary comment that life there was cosier than in the trenches. The peak year for families housed in the Hutments was 1923 with 137 in residence totalling 600 persons but by 1928 this had dwindled to 22 family groups.

Conditions at the Hutments left much to be desired. Most of the huts were 24 feet long by 10 feet wide however some were smaller and when divided a family would have just 120 square feet of living space! Dividing partitions were of blockwork to ceiling height only. Noise transfer through the thin boarded ceilings afforded minimal privacy. Cold water was available at an outside standpipe, with one to every five huts. Warmth was obtained from a single slow combustion stove. Slops were emptied into open gulleys. Laundering was carried out by rota in the communal wash houses, many women rose at 4.00 am in the morning to light solid fuel boilers when on "Early Turn". Queues often formed to use the six coppers (boilers) between the two wash houses. The toilets were in blocks, 18 for men and 22 for women, and according to the Sanitary Inspector's report in 1921 were "In poor condition and often fouled". The windows and doors fitted badly and many of the huts were damp. By 1923 the huts were looking shabby and painting was urgently needed. Permission to keep chickens and other animals was refused by the council but it was noted that there was a significant "Dog" problem.

In April 1920 it became necessary to pull down eight huts, seven of which were occupied plus part of the large officers recreation building measuring 161 by 29 feet to enable new houses to be built. Twenty of the new houses were to be offered to the hut dwellers. The Borough Accountant proposed to use part of the hut to store bathing tents and deckchairs in winter at Churchdale Road. The 11th Eastbourne Scout

Green Street Farm smallholdings 1961 (Mrs D Collins)

troop requested the remainder as a headquarters but the request was refused. It was offered for sale but there were no takers. Some of the huts were sold off and made useful homes on the Smallholdings above Green Street Farm. Mrs E Williamson owner of the York House Hotel bought two huts and installed them on a site on the Hastings road near the Langney Priory. The conversions were a model, each hut was equipped with a kitchen, bathroom, and running water and were intended for farm workers. The conversions merited a full description in the Eastbourne edition of The Sussex Express in January 1921. These privately funded alterations costing significantly more than the Council afforded for the Hutments in Victoria Drive. The huts at Langney survived until displaced by post 1945 Council housing.

As the Old Town Council estate developed with the construction of Victoria Gardens, Victoria Road and Beechy Avenue, together with the southern portions of Royal Sussex Crescent and Command Road it became necessary to demolish the Hutments by stages. By 1932 these developments were complete, the only reminders today of this temporary township are the foundations of some of the huts found by residents when gardening and by the commemorative road names Command Road and Cavalry Crescent. Green Street Farm stretched from Victoria Drive towards the foot of the Downs. The farm buildings were located where today South Avenue joins The Crescent. The farm gave its name to the private development carried out in the 1960s on the post 1918 smallholdings close to the Downs.

Open Air - Downs School

In July 1919 it was agreed by the Council that six huts on the south-western boundary of the former Cavalry Command Depot should be allocated to an open air school at a cost of £2,400 including equipment. At the time, fresh air and sunshine were recommended by the medical profession as beneficial, in the treatment of rickets and skeletal Tuberculosis. The school opened on 7th June 1920 to meet the needs of delicate children and those with physical defects. Pictures taken in 1926 show children taking outdoor naps and having lessons in the open air but with the huts in a poor state. The huts survived in use at the school until 1935 when they were replaced with brick built pavilions. The last hut to be used for this purpose was pulled down in 1936. The name of the school changed in 1959 to the Downs School and it continues to this day providing education for children with moderate learning difficulties.

Children at lessons Open Air School 1929

Children at rest Open Air school 1929

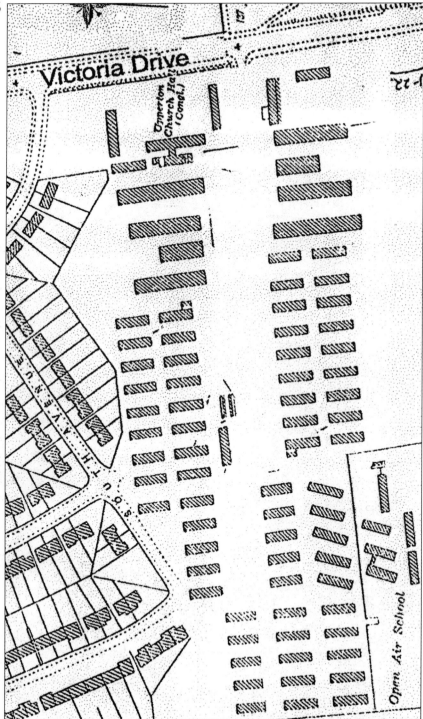

76

Victoria Drive

Site of Cavalry Command Depot OS map LXX9NW 1/250 1925

Open Air School

8. LAW and DISORDER

The Eastbourne Police Force had come into existence in 1898 and despite the wartime challenges independently maintain the King's peace, with from time to time help from the army Provost Corps who were stationed at The Redoubt. A refusal by the Council in January 1915 to issue bus passes to military policemen was regretted subsequently after a late night assault on a bus conductor.

AIR RAIDS.
POLICE WARNING.

In view of the possibility of attacks by hostile aircraft, the Chief Constable of Eastbourne deems it advisable again to recommend residents if such attacks are made here to remain under cover, and to keep a supply of water and sand readily available to deal with incendiary fires. This opportunity is taken of suggesting that chemical liquid fire extinguishers should not be purchased without a written guarantee that they comply with the specification of the Board of Trade, Office of Works, or some approved Fire Prevention Committee.

Many dry powder fire extinguishers are much advertised. The Chief Constable warns the public, as the result of experiments made by a competent Committee of Experts, that no reliance can be placed upon such appliances for effectively controlling fires such as are likely to be caused by bombs, explosive or incendiary. The Chief Constable is advised as the result of these experiments that the provision, and prompt and intelligent use, of water or of sand or of both in dealing with such outbreaks of fire is the best, simplest and most economical safeguard.

EDWARD J. J. TEALE, Major,
Chief Constable of the Borough
of Eastbourne.
30th September, 1915.

Air Raid Notice

Members of police forces were often drawn from the ranks of ex-regular soldiers who were reservists liable to recall to the army in an emergency. At the outbreak of war the strength of the force totalled 96 men, by November 1915 thirty-three had joined the colours one having been killed in action. The Chief Constable, Major E J Teale, reported that three more men could be spared but no more. Earlier a call had been made for special constables and employers were asked to provide names of employees who could serve at a ratio of one in five of their staff. The original intention was for the constables to look after their own premises. The watchmen who guarded the waterworks were also to be sworn in as special constables, 150 armbands at ninepence each were ordered for them. The special constables remained as a force, 197 strong, until disbanded on 20th June 1919.

In March 1915 Miss Brodie Hall sought permission to set up an Eastbourne branch of the Women's Patrol Committee to look after the interests of girls between the age of 14 and 17 years. It was agreed for a trial period with the members numbering 42.

Ordnance Yard venue for Courts martial

The Chief Constable issued instructions on 14th January 1915 regarding air raids. "If an explosion takes place the nearest constable must proceed immediately to the scene, he must summon the fire brigade, ambulances and doctors. He must also notify the nearest Police Station and ask for two hand lamps to be sent". At the time there were three Police Stations for the town, Grove Road, Latimer Road and Amber Lodge, Rosebery Avenue, Hampden Park. Warnings of air raids were customarily given by Police Constables blowing whistles and carrying a sign with the words "Air Raid".

On 19th August 1915 it was announced that war damage insurance for the owners of property had become obligatory, the rate for aerial attack was two shillings per cent and for the additional cover of bombardment from the sea, the rate would be three shillings per cent. This followed the German naval bombardment of East Coast towns which commenced in December 1914 and ended in 1917 by which time 12 bombardments had taken place. The air attacks commenced with Zeppelin airship raids on the East Coast and London. Later, bombing planes took part making over 100 raids on the same targets. In June 1917 concern was expressed about the efficacy of the air raid warnings after a recent raid on Folkestone.

A possible German invasion was a threat that persisted throughout the war. Harrowing tales were reported in 1914 of the Belgian and French populations which took to the roads as refugees, accordingly instructions were laid down for an orderly evacuation if the enemy should land. As early as January 1915 the Invasion Committee were asking for instructions to be published.

These instructions would have included the following: -

Church bells will be rung as a signal for evacuation

1. Everyone should run to their homes and put on as much warm clothes and underclothing as they can. A top coat should be put on and one rolled blanket with the ends tied with string should be carried over one shoulder.

2. Bring such food that might be in the house, bread, cheese and cooked meat that can easily be carried, also one cooking pot, kettle or saucepan for each member of a family and one mug.

3. Proceed to the parish meeting point and wait for orders from the head special constable.

4. On arrival at the place to which they are removed they will be instructed. The positions which they must occupy.

Householders were told to leave doors unlocked as less damage would be caused by the enemy when they entered homes.

From time to time bombing practice would take place. In May 1918 residents were asking for additional notice to be given at police stations and on the Parades in addition to newspaper advertisements of such happenings.

Lighting restrictions and their enforcement gave the police and the courts much additional work. Orders had been made in April 1915 regarding lighting restrictions in coastal areas from Northumberland to Dorset. The blackout was not so strict as in the Second World War. Reduced intensity street lighting was permitted. Many of the street lamps were fitted with blue shades. By June 1916 the Council reported that 212 street lamps, 102 arc and 110 incandescent, were too strong to be used in wartime. The festoon lights and every other standard lamp along the promenade were also extinguished for the duration of the war. Shopkeepers were allowed to use low intensity lighting for window displays. Householders were forbidden to allow lights to show from windows, infringements were followed by prosecutions, several hundred being brought during the course of the war with fines of ten shillings or up to £2 for repeated offences. During the winter of 1917 it was proposed to have 50 lamps lit on the unlit bus routes. Twenty-six gas lamps were to be converted to electricity so that the ten-minute extinguishing rule in case of an air raid could be implemented.

In December 1918 full shop window lighting was allowed for Christmas. Early in May 1919 special permission was given to relax the lighting restrictions over the Peace Day celebration period and by the end of May all the lighting restrictions were permanently removed.

The large influx of young soldiers into the town, many away from the constraints of their home environment, often lead to excessive drinking and roistering. In September 1917 a bus inspector was assaulted at the railway station by soldiers who gave false names, the Council then asked the Camp Commanding Officers to provide Military Police at the station from 8.00 pm to 10.00 pm each evening. Colonel Follett, of the Cavalry Command Depot, offered to place a Military Policeman on each bus during that period.

Before the Courts

10th October 1914 A case of alleged deception came before the Lewes Magistrates concerning meat supplies for men of the South Wales Borderers' Regiment stationed in the Old Naval Prison, Lewes. An Eastbourne butcher had been contracted to supply meat to the cookhouse. A consignment of 140 pounds of meat found its way to an address in St Leonards instead of Lewes. It was suggested by the defence that the labels had fallen off during the journey and had accidentally been changed in a van on the way to the railway station. The case was discharged as it was uncertain if a genuine labelling mistake had occurred.

10th February 1915 A cabman Matthew B------ of Gaudick Mews was before the court on charges of receiving War Office Oats. Private Clement Hockey of the Hampshire Carabineers in camp at Willingdon, and the cabman were found guilty of handling stolen property, sacks of oats were found in the cab and at the accused's address more empty sacks were discovered. The soldier would be tried by court martial and the cabman was convicted receiving three months imprisonment with hard labour.

10th March 1915 At Lewes Assizes Alfred S------ a bricklayer was convicted of assaulting Sergeant Hahn, a Military Policeman, at Willingdon, the accused was given six months hard labour.

31st March 1915 Lieutenant William C---- hit a lamp post at the Junction of Victoria Place and Grand Parade whilst driving a motorcycle sidecar combination. He was given first aid and subsequently taken to the Military Hospital at the Ordnance Yard. Later he was convicted of riding at an excessive speed and was fined £2:12 shillings including costs.

14th April 1915 A deserter from the Loyal North Lancashire Regiment was apprehended in civilian clothes in Seaside Road. Private A Chester H---- was found in a drunken and disorderly state, his uniform and papers had been found in a bundle at the back of Rylstone Road. He was remanded in custody to await escort back to his unit on Salisbury Plain.

21st April 1915 Alfonds de W----- a Belgian refugee of Langney Road was found drunk and disorderly in Queens Gardens. A plea that he was unused to strong English beer allowed him to escape with a five shilling fine and the cost of a taxi fare.

25th April 1915 Private William Owen J------ a deserter from the Lancashire Fusiliers was charged with abducting a 17 year old girl Miss Jessie G-----from a house in Langney Road. He had been billeted there from 7th December 1914 to 4th March 1915 when he went missing with the girl. They first stayed at a boarding house in Hampden Park posing as a married couple. The couple then moved on to Hailsham where they obtained work at an hotel, he as a groom the girl as a domestic. The girl was fired for disobedience, the pair then went to London staying in a hotel as a married couple. The defendant told the girl that he had £200 in a Liverpool Savings bank and would need to travel there in order to withdraw it. On the train he was seen and recognised by a member of his unit who denounced him to two officers also travelling on the train. The officers had the deserter arrested by the Military Police. The Magistrates committed the man to the Assizes on the abduction charge and after any civil sentence had been served he would be dealt with by the military. The accused had the last words with "A spell in prison would be better than getting killed in France". Their last night's hotel bill had not been paid, between them the couple had one shilling when arrested.

19th June 1915 A collection of 23 blackout offences was heard, mostly receiving a 10 shilling fine.

23rd June 1915 A mysterious case under the Defence of the Realm Acts came before the magistrates. A Private James on duty with the 5th

Redoubt H Q of the military police and town guardroom

Scottish Rifles was posting a letter when he was offered a certain article by a civilian. The court then went into camera and the civilian was convicted and given three-month's hard labour. It is conjectured that the "Article offered" might have been a seditious tract.

21st July 1915 Private Wallis S--------, 5th Scottish Rifles before the court for Drunken and Disorderly behaviour.

28th July 1915 Another 16 blackout cases before the court.

28th July 1915 Private Walter S------, 5th Scottish Rifles stationed at Birling Gap was found drunk and disorderly in Camp, he was disobedient and refused to obey orders. He was sent to the Ordnance Yard for Court-Martial.

4th August 1915 Richard I------ was seen at Beachy Head by a member of the 5th Scottish Rifles on guard duty. The accused was told that he was in a prohibited area and that he must leave at once. At the time of the offence he was wearing uniform and with an Imperial Service Badge and a slouch hat. He claimed to have served with the Canadian army in the Boer War. He was convicted of wearing a uniform with intent to deceive and it was disclosed that he was not entitled to wear the badge. The uniform should have been returned to the 2nd Hove Battalion of the Voluntary Training Corps when he resigned. He was sentenced to 14 days hard labour.

22nd September 1915 Two local butchers were before the court regarding the inadequate meat content of sausages offered for sale. Mr Chitty of Junction Road was discharged after the analyst changed his testimony stating that he had inadvertently reversed the bread and meat content of 38 and 62 per cent respectively at the first hearing. Mr B---- of Seaside Road was fined. Analysis of his sausages revealed the percentage content as water 47, fat 13, and bread 15 meat 25.

13th October 1915 Private James M----- 2nd Battalion Royal Irish Rifles age 30 was charged with bigamously marrying Kate Hilda G------ on 9th August whilst his wife was still alive. The accused had been a patient at Summerdown Camp and had deserted, he went up to a Police Constable with his "Wife" and confessed.

20th October 1915 Private James C------ of the Army Service Corps was seen to be driving an army lorry furiously in Terminus Road and the Station yard. When stopped by a constable he refused to give his name or produce a driving licence. Later the constable visited Summerdown Camp and found the accused who again refused to produce a licence and offered to take the constable to Colonel Bostock, the Commanding Officer. The constable was led right through the camp and pointed in the direction of the Downs and told to keep going until he reached Brighton and that he, the constable, should be at the front in France and not wasting his time in Eastbourne. Later Colonel Bostock told the constable that an army permit to drive was sufficient. In court the defendant and his Colonel were told that the War Office had decreed that all army drivers in England must have a licence. The defendant was fined £5 for abuse, obstruction and offence to the constable. Colonel Bostock stated that he was in France when the War Office order was issued regarding driving licences. The defendant was unable to pay so the Colonel had to stand surety for the fine.

8th January 1916 Two vehicles were seen racing along the Sea Front, a lorry belonging to the Army Service Corps and a light ambulance when a collision occurred between the ambulance, and a baked potato barrow. The barrow boy was knocked over and slightly hurt. In court it was stated that one of the drivers had previously received a caution. Privates John P----- the ambulance driver and Anthony H---- the lorry driver both of Broomfield Street were fined 50 shillings each.

19th February 1916 Mary Mc ---- of Langney Road was before the court for concealing a deserter, Private John Guy of the 11th Loyal North Lancashire Regiment, the accused was sentenced to seven days in prison. The concealment would have been for a period of at least nine months, as the regiment left the town for Salisbury Plain in April 1915.

27th April 1917 The Council prosecuted a local trader for the unlawful use of the Red Cross emblem, the case was dismissed on a plea of ignorance of the regulations by the accused.

4th August 1918 Private William John M------, Labour Battalion attached to the Cavalry Command Depot, Victoria Drive, was before the court charged with obstructing the Police. A man was being arrested for drunk and disorderly behaviour at the rear of the Burlington Hotel when the defendant sought to free the man from the arresting officers. Private M----- was convicted and received two months prison with hard labour.

31st July 1918 The White Corner Restaurant, where the Co-op now stands, at the corner of Victoria Place, was fined for serving an illegal meal. An inspector had purchased a trial meal and found that he had been served with more than the permitted amount of bread and cake at one sitting, namely one and a half ounces.

25th August 1918 Two more cases under food control regulations came before the court the first of sugar hoarding. A local housewife who applied legally for a special allowance of 41 pounds of sugar for jam making was visited by a food inspector. No evidence of jam making was found nor were there any fruit trees present in her garden as had been claimed on the application form. The second related to a greengrocer who gave an address in Arundel Road who was caught selling haricot beans for eightpence a pound instead of the controlled price of sevenpence.

22nd September 1918 A Polegate man was stopped when driving in Elm Grove Brighton to the racecourse. He was prosecuted for the mis-use of petrol. In his defence he stated that when he set out he had no intention of going to the races but found himself going in that direction. He was fined £2 or 11 days in prison in default.

13th October 1918 A local tradesman, Justice of the Peace and Councillor was summoned for distributing unsolicited business catalogues in breach of paper saving orders. The case was discharged as not proven.

16th November 1918 A case came before the court a breach for the "No Treating Order". This order had been made to discourage excessive drinking and eventually licensing hours were introduced for public houses and other establishments where alcoholic drinks were sold and consumed.

22nd January 1919 A nurse working at the De Walden Court Red Cross Hospital was convicted of stealing a gold watch from a colleague, the accused Kathleen Mc N----- admitted to being a drug taker and was bound over for 12 months.

26th February 1919 Although the Armistice was in force food restrictions continued to the extent that 11 local butchers were fined for selling meat in excess of ration coupons.

30th April 1919 A Canadian soldier was fined £1 for being found drunk and disorderly. This was the last wartime misdemeanour to come before the courts.

9. MISADVENTURE

Military activity behind the front lines can bring its life threatening situations. Although not as challenging as being in the front line a careless or misjudged action can cost lives. Accidental deaths, civilian or military would require the attention of His Majesty's Coroner for East Sussex, Mr Vere Benson. Censorship especially in the early days of the war was not as strict as it might have been. Court cases concerning servicemen often gave details of the units to which they belonged and provide useful clues to historians trying to piece together unit locations. Over 100 patients died in the Eastbourne Military Hospitals during the war-time period. Most of these were battlefield casualties which would not have required the Coroner's attention unless the death occurred as the result of an operative procedure. The 1918 influenza pandemic victims did not reach a formal inquest. The flying services casualties are listed under the two establishments. Traffic accidents reflected the transport modes of the times, whilst motor accidents predominate, horse drawn transport could be equally deadly.

30th January 1915 Private G Strachan 13th Battalion Manchester Regiment knocked down by a runaway horse in Cornfield Road received facial injuries and was taken to Urmston Red Cross Hospital, where he recovered. Private W Ross Loyal North Lancashire Regiment cycled into a wall in Enys Road. He recovered in the Princess Alice Hospital.

3rd March 1915 A barmaid, Miss Lily Goble aged 24, employed at the Albion Hotel was crossing the road at Victoria Place with a friend Miss Agnes Leonard. An army motorcyclist, Sergeant Pearson 10th Loyal North Lancashire Regiment, usually on Military Police duty at the Redoubt, collided with Miss Goble. One of Messrs Bassett's cars took the victim to hospital where she was found to be dead on arrival. Sergeant Pearson was taken to the Military Hospital at the Ordnance Yard with a fractured leg. At subsequent court hearings it emerged that the motorcyclist did not have a licence, and was not authorised to use the machine. Sergeant Pearson was making a journey from the Redoubt to the orderly room of the Manchester Regiment 65th Brigade in Grange Road. Witnesses stated that speed was excessive, at least 30 mph. The magistrates remanded him to Lewes assizes on a manslaughter charge but he was subsequently acquitted.

6th March 1915 Private Gorman, Kings Liverpool Regiment, was found drunk in the Redoubt Gardens. He was taken to the Military Hospital at the Ordnance Yard where he died. It was discovered that he had drunk at least a pint of whisky before collapsing.

24th March 1915 An accident occurred in Grand Parade at the junction of St Aubyns Road when a collision took place between a taxi driven by Robert Stroud of Bexhill and an army sergeant who was a pedestrian. The accident happened at 8.55 pm under conditions of reduced street lighting. Captain Wilton Schiff of the 13th Royal Battalion Sussex Regiment from Cooden Camp, who was accompanied by a lady, were the passengers who were unhurt. The injured man Sergeant Bennett was taken to the Wish Rocks Red Cross Hospital with a broken leg and facial injuries.

24th April 1915 An accident occurred at the Whitbread Hollow RAMC Camp which resulted in fatal injuries to Private Alfred Belton of the 64th Field Ambulance RAMC. A water cart weighing one ton ran away down a slope and the wheels passed over him when he attempted to stop it. A fatigue party of 10 had been mustered to move the cart but Belton and another man had started off without waiting for the rest of the party and were unable to control its movement.

8th May 1915 Mr William Body, a bricklayer, employed by William Arrol and Company, was working at the Polegate Airship Station constructing the airship sheds. He was standing two feet above the ground on a trestle during a winching operation on a second trestle. The trestles were 60 feet tall and weighed five tons, a gust of wind caught the trestle snapping the cable which had a breaking strain of 15 tons. The unfortunate man was crushed receiving fatal injuries.

26th May 1915 At 11.15pm just after the street lights were extinguished, Ernest Chinnery aged 37 of Willowfield Road was driving towards Beachy Head. He was employed by Bovill's Garage opposite the Albion Hotel as a taxi driver. Mr Chinnery was killed instantly when his Fiat taxi was in a head on collision with a converted Talbot wagonette weighing one and a half tons belonging to the Royal Naval Air Service. This was being driven by a duty Flight Lieutenant Jones in the direction of the Pier. The taxi passengers a Lieutenant and a Miss B----- age 16 of Pevensey Road had been to the Hippodrome and were travelling to Summerdown Camp. It took four hours to separate the vehicles and clear the road.

16th June 1915 A Miss Marion Gregson, aged 36, had never fully recovered from diphtheria contracted whilst in China, had received treatment at a number of clinics for depressive illness. A taxi driver from Baker Street, London gave evidence of the hiring of his cab to come to Eastbourne, the deceased asked to travel to Birling Gap. Fusilier Robert McKenzie, 5th Scottish Rifles (Cameronians), on guard duty at Birling Gap warned her that it was a prohibited place and that trench digging was taking place and that she should leave forthwith. Later the soldier saw her jump from the Seven Sisters, a wristwatch was found at the cliff edge. A suicide verdict was returned.

23rd June 1915 A party of officers and ladies making a journey in a Ford car were involved in a collision at the junction of Grange and Blackwater Roads. Two of the party were treated at the Wish Rocks Red Cross Hospital, one with bruises the other with a broken leg.

4th August 1915 Private James Bond 72nd Field Ambulance a strong swimmer was acting as an out post lifeguard for an organised bathing party at Holywell. The officer in charge had called and whistled him to return nearer the shore to no avail. The body clad in swimming trunks and plimsolls was recovered one week later at Hastings. The inquest was told that a safety boat could not be used as it was leaking and awaiting repairs.

3rd November 1915 Lieutenant and Mrs St John Simpson had been married a week and were spending their honeymoon at the Queens Hotel. They had recently jointly purchased a new American two seater car which on the day in question had been taken for a drive to Beachy Head. As the road was narrow the car had been parked on the grass at the roadside 250

Remains of the American two seater recovered from Beachy Head (Brit Lib)

yards east of the Belle Tout Lighthouse and 45 yards from the cliff edge. They both got out of the car to inspect the lighthouse but found it locked. Mrs Simpson returned to the car whilst her husband answered a call of nature in the bushes. Lieutenant Simpson told the inquest that he was horrified to see that the car had disappeared, and could not recall if he saw it go over the cliff edge or not. He was taken to Hodcombe Farm cottages nearby in a state of shock. Private Gibson of the 5th Scottish Rifles heard the crash and was sent down to the beach to investigate the wreck, he reported that the deceased was lying outside the car still holding her handbag. The inquest was told that the car was in gear and had an electric starter. A verdict of accidental death was returned. Messrs Lovely's Cavendish Place garage recovered the car by dismantling it and hauling it up the cliff at Birling Gap.

1st December 1915 A car driven by an experienced chauffeur with two nurses and three children as passengers skidded in Seaside and hit a cast iron high tension electricity junction box. The shaken passengers were assisted from the wreckage and taken into a nearby house. A number of men attempted to move the car from the remains of the junction box, but in so doing the rear axle touched a live cable. Private Thomas Marshall of the RAMC and Mr E Shadwell of Dudley Road an employee of Samuel Bradford, Coal Merchant were immediately electrocuted "As if struck by lightning". A message was sent to the power station in Corporation Road (Churchdale Road) asking for the current to be turned off. The generating attendant mistakenly shut down the entire plant completely blacking out the town and several hours elapsed before the supply was restored. This event occurred long before the days of the National Grid and electricity supplies were generated locally without backup from outside sources. The local press singled out that the most newsworthy effect was the interruption to the Sunday afternoon concert on the Pier organised by Miss Margaret Cooper in the Theatre. Miss Gladys Mitchell's solo continued once candles had been lit.

18th June 1916 Horses and mules were much used in the services and brought their own hazards to the handlers. Driver Abel Mankello, aged 25, of the 2nd Home Counties Brigade, Sussex Royal Field Artillery, stationed at Brasted, Kent received a kick on the head as he was attempting to harness a mule. Despite being attended to by the unit medical officer for superficial wounds his condition deteriorated rapidly. He was admitted to the Sevenoaks Red Cross Hospital at Chipstead where he died of Meningitis. Driver Mankellow's home was at 187 Seaside and he was buried at Ocklynge on 5th August.

14th April 1917 Private Winchester Army Service Corps who came from Bristol was attached to the 13th Devonshire Regiment. Soldiers were used to replace agricultural workers who had been called into the army. Private Winchester was working on a haystack at Michelham Priory cutting out mouldy hay with a long handled knife. He got too near the edge of the stack and fell off becoming trapped in the baling machine. He was taken to the Central Military Hospital, Church Street where he died from his injuries.

4th August 1917 A love triangle at Seaford had fatal results when Private Joseph Wild of the 29th Canadian Battalion died in All Saints Hospital. Private Wild had been shot by a Montenegrin subject who was caught and sent for trial at Lewes Assizes where he was convicted of manslaughter and sentenced to 3 years imprisonment.

4th October 1917 Sergeant William Hoddell of the Canadian Army stationed at Seaford slipped on some stone stairs at Seaford receiving head injuries from which he died in All Saints Hospital.

8th May 1918 Three Canadian soldiers on a motorcycle sidecar combination were seen to be driving erratically down the Goffs on a wet morning. At the junction with Upperton Road the machine tipped over throwing the occupants into the road. Dr Muir Smith, a local Doctor, attended the scene and the injured men were taken to the Central Military Hospital.   Lance Corporal S Scanes, aged 42, of the 6th Canadian Reserve Pioneers, East Ontario Regiment, died from his injuries and was buried in Ocklynge Cemetery.

16th May 1918 Private L Peever 6th Reserve Battalion Canadian Infantry (Eastern Ontario Regiment), aged 22, received an accidental gunshot wounds at Seaford Camp and died in All Saints Hospital. He is buried in Seaford Cemetery.

26th June 1918 Private James Callicham died in All Saints Hospital following surgery after being kicked on the head by a horse at Seaford. Camp.

24th July 1918 Ordnance accidents in training were unusual until the latter years of the war for the simple reason that the early volunteers in and around Eastbourne did not have uniforms let alone weapons.   Sergeant G H Tipper 1st Canadian Infantry (Western Ontario Regiment) died of wounds in All Saints Hospital. He was fatally injured whilst demonstrating a detonator to troops at Seaford Camp. He is buried in Seaford Cemetery.

2nd November 1918 Albert Edward Lower, aged 56, of Bradford Street died in The Princess Alice Hospital after falling through a corrugated asbestos roof at the Cavalry Command Depot, Victoria Drive. He was carrying a bucket of cement whilst walking without support boards on a roof. He fell through landing amongst a group of officers. He was given first aid and died of a fractured skull in the Princess Alice Hospital.

22nd November 1918 Private Thomas Liebrecht, aged 25, of 4th Queens Own Hussars from Dublin died in the Central Military Hospital after being injured at Chiddingly in a motor cycle accident.

12th February 1919 An 11 year old boy Frederick Warner of Dennis Road, now renamed Dursley Road, met with an accident in Whitley Road. A RAF motor tender was carrying a party of officers from St Anthony's Hill aerodrome to the Mess at South Lynn. The boy was seen hanging on the back of a greengrocer's lorry. He let go and ran across the road in front of the RAF tender which could not avoid him, with fatal results.

21st May 1919 A Canadian Ambulance seen driving down Church Street at a fast speed, it swerved to avoid a bus and collided with the corner of the Lamb Inn before overturning. The ambulance was taking 7 passengers from Seaford to the Central Hospital, some of them were hurt in the accident and required treatment. As the accident occurred at a point past the hospital it had either lost its way or experienced a brake failure.

10. A PLAGUE OF U-BOATS

Peacetime shipping losses in the two main sea areas off Eastbourne, the Royal Sovereign and Beachy Head, amounted to just six vessels in the period 1900-1914. Enemy action began against shipping in March 1915 and continued unabated until November 1918. During this period 57 ships were sunk by enemy action. Three were from neutral countries, Holland, Spain and Norway the rest were under British or allied flags.

Britain had enjoyed maritime supremacy after the final defeat of Napoleon. Her merchant fleet, the largest in the world, was protected by the Royal Navy, the most powerful fleet in history. The Imperial German Navy had sought to equal and if possible surpass the supremacy of the Royal Navy. Both had developed submarines into effective weapons of somewhat limited range. Britain regarded the submarine as a minor part of the navy, Germany however regarded the U-boat arm as a major striking force. German U-boats could reach Scapa Flow, the main British base, and range throughout the Channel. On 22nd September 1914, the U-9 attacked and sank three British Cruisers Aboukir, Houge and Cressy in the southern North Sea with the loss of 1,459 lives.

Ships passing Beachy Head would usually steam in close to land to pass the prominence. This would be a good area for a U-boat to lie in wait for victims. Thirty-seven ships were sunk in the vicinity of Beachy Head, the remaining 20 were lost near The Royal Sovereign light vessel. Between 27th February and 5th April 1915 no fewer than 14 merchant vessels encountered German submarines with varying results. These sinkings were surprisingly reported in some detail by the local newspapers thereby giving the enemy valuable confirmation of its activities. After 5th April 1915 a censorship blackout was imposed on reports of these attacks.

The sinkings often came in batches. Post-war captured German records confirmed the identity of the U-boat Captain and his ship's number. The methods used by the U-boats varied. Often the U-boat would surface and fire a warning shot to stop the ship, the crew would be ordered away in the ships boats, interrogated, and the ship would then be sunk with a torpedo. Smaller ships would be stopped in the same way but the crew would be required to ferry a boarding party to the victim so that food and valuables might be ransacked before scuttling charges would be placed. On other occasions shellfire would be used to sink the ship. With this type of sinking there was little loss of life. Torpedoes fired without warning from submerged submarines or ships striking mines laid by submarines were at greater risk of crew losses from the explosion.

These ships in distress would call for assistance by firing rockets, Wireless Telegraphy being of recent introduction would only be found in larger vessels. Neighbouring ships would proceed to the sinking not unusually being the U-boat's next victim. Naval patrols would often come to the rescue as would the Eastbourne and Newhaven Lifeboats. From January 1917 Germany commenced unrestricted submarine warfare which meant the sinking without warning of any ship thought to be serving the allied interest. This decision is reflected in the following table of local sinkings.

Year	Ships lost	Tonnage
1914	nil	nil
1915	14	36,383
1916	12	37,308
1917	25	65,844
1918	8	28,749

The Admiralty had steadfastly refused to provide escorts for merchant shipping apart from cross Channel Troop Transports, until May 1917 when the Prime Minister, Mr Lloyd George, imposed this requirement on the Admiralty. Until then the only deterrents were the Naval seaplane Patrols from Newhaven and

the airships from Polegate. Both were relatively slow and their approach
was heralded by engine noise giving an alert U-boat time to submerge.

The ships varied in size from 116 to 11,000 tons, eight belonged to the
Royal Navy, mainly requisitioned trawlers being used as minesweepers.
Four larger ships were carrying Government stores to France. The rest
were an indicator of Britain's widespread maritime trade, 13 colliers from
South Wales and North East Coast ports, a tanker, a ship carrying bones
and another with a cargo of manure. Rice from Siam, oranges from
Spain, hides from West Africa and phosphates from Tunisia all went to
the bottom of the sea. Eleven empty ships in ballast were also sunk
whilst the grand total included four sailing ships two Barques and two
Brigantines. Crews were rescued on most occasions but nine sinkings
were attended by the loss of 147 lives.

The first ship to be lost off the town was the **Branksome Chine**, a
collier, was sunk by the U-8 on 23rd February 1915. The vessel had just
left Newhaven when she was hit 14 miles SSE of Beachy Head, the crew
of 20 escaped in the ship's boats. The **SS Cairntorr**, owned by Cairns
Noble of Newcastle, with 3,500 tons of coal bound for Genoa went
down in three hours after being torpedoed by the U-34, on 21st March
1915, eight miles ESE of Beachy Head. Eighteen of the crew of 33 was
brought ashore at Eastbourne Pier and accommodated overnight at the
Albion and Albermarle Hotels, the rest of the crew were taken to
Newhaven. Four local pleasure motor boats including Mr Boniface's **Star
of Peace** and John Huggett's **Royal Sovereign** assisted with the rescue.

Rescues of crew members of sunken ships were undertaken variously by
naval vessels, other merchant ships and the local lifeboats. The
Newhaven lifeboat was better able to effect rescues than the Eastbourne
boat because it was motor powered. The Eastbourne station would have
to wait until 1921 before its pulling boat with an auxiliary sail, the James
Stevens No 6, was replaced by a motor boat. Often when called out on
a rescue mission the motor pleasure boats the **Bonnie Charlie** owned by

Henry Boniface and the **Estella** belonging to the Hardy brothers would tow the lifeboat, under coxswain, Tim Erridge, to the scene. The Eastbourne lifeboat participated in six rescues in the first three months of 1915. Rescues had their own elements of danger, as a submarine would await submerged for a rescue vessel to stop and would then sink the rescuer. On 20th May 1917 the **Porthkerry**, 1,920 tons stopped to pick up the survivors of the **Tycho**, 3,216 tons when the UB-40 fired again sinking the rescue ship.

SS Thordis rammed and disabled U-6 (Aust Agder Muset Arenal Norway)

On 28th February 1915 the **SS Thordis**, 500 tons, on a voyage from Blyth to Plymouth with a cargo of coal, was attacked by the U-6, about 10 miles off Beachy Head. Earlier James Prodger a local fisherman out in a whelk boat had seen a submarine on the surface. The master of the Thordis, Captain J W Bell, noticed a periscope 30 yards away, he called for full speed which was ten knots and as he did so a torpedo was fired but missed. When the submarine's periscope re-appeared the ship's captain turned towards it and felt a bump as the ship hit the U-boat and an oil slick appeared. The captain's action was fêted in the newspapers at the time and he was subsequently given the rank of Commander, Royal Naval Reserve, a Distinguished Service Cross and £200. The captain and crew shared monetary rewards from both the Admiralty and a leading newspaper. When the ship completed her voyage and was examined at Saltash by divers it was felt that a "kill" had not been made. After the war it was confirmed that the U-6 returned to her home port, under Oberleutnant Lepsius, with a badly damaged conning tower and with both periscopes destroyed.

On 26th July 1917 the U-65 commanded by Kapitan Leutenant Otto Steinbuck scored a notable success off the Royal Sovereign shoal. This was to be his 100th victory. HMS Ariadne was one of eight ships of the Diadem class of protected cruisers of 11,000 tons built in 1896 at Clydebank, a coal burner with reciprocating engines. By the outbreak of war she was outdated, and her machinery and boilers were worn out, even when new her massive armour plating slowed her to a maximum of 20 knots. The vessel carried sixteen six inch guns and twelve 12 pounders. In order to give her a useful existence she had been converted to a minelayer with a capacity of 400 mines.

On the afternoon of 24th July she had left her home port of Immingham bound for Plymouth where it was planned to extend the deep minefield protecting the port. No route instructions were given to Captain Harry Hesketh-Smyth other than to contact the Vice-Admiral at Dover. The ship left the Humber early, in so doing failed to collect mails and signal orders dated a week earlier. These orders required a wireless watch on "Q" wavelength instead of "S" wavelength. The Ariadne listened on the wrong frequency and consequently failed to receive submarine warning reports. Whilst at anchor in the Downs, a stretch of water off Deal, orders were received to take a route past Beachy Head to a point three miles south of Brighton avoiding a known danger area. On the morning of 26th July a submarine was reported off Beachy Head and although the

Admiral at Dover knew that it was close to Ariadne's route no warning was given to the ship. It was not the practice to warn ships in the Downs of submarines off Beachy Head.

HMS Ariadne torpedoed off the Royal Sovereign (Maritime Inf Cent)

The Ariadne delayed by fog weighed anchor at 10.30 am passed Folkestone and then proceeded down the mine swept channel accompanied by 2 destroyers HMS **Peregrine** and HMS **Norman**. At 2.07 pm the C-in-C Portsmouth signalled that an enemy submarine had been sighted 5 miles WSW of the Royal Sovereign Light, this warning went unheard in the Ariadne's wireless cabin. At 2.22 pm a violent explosion shook the vessel, a torpedo had exploded in the "C" boiler room which soon flooded giving the ship a 10 degree list. The engine and boiler rooms were evacuated, with the starboard engine stopped, the port engine still running and the helm jammed hard a port, the ship circled for 25 minutes until the port engine also stopped. A paddle minesweeper had taken the Ariadne in tow when at 3.12 pm a second torpedo exploded in "B" boiler room. Immediately the ship began to capsize and the captain ordered "Every man for himself". Of the complement, 384 men were saved and 33 lost, some of the survivors were brought ashore at Eastbourne Pier. At the time of the second attack there were four paddle minesweepers and three trawlers in attendance but nothing was seen of the enemy submarine although the tracks of both torpedoes had been seen. At the subsequent court-martial Captain Smyth was exonerated.

The wreck constituted a significant risk for shipping being just below the surface at low water. Demolition of the wreck was undertaken by the Ocean Salvage and Towing Company and would extend over 4 summers from 1919. The work involved placing charges of one ton of explosive by divers and detonating the charge electrically. The explosive charge of the mines would have combined with destructive effect. The work gave additional employment to the local boatmen and the resultant explosions were heard over a wide area of the town. Today the remains of the wreck are categorised as a war grave covered by the provisions of the Protection of Military Remains Act 1986.

The last recorded sinking in the area was that of the SS **Moldavia** a trooper of 9,000 tons, from the United States carrying American troops bound for France which was torpedoed by the U-57. Most of the crew and the troops were rescued, many of the injured being taken to Newhaven, in all 56 lives were lost. This was the only major loss at sea out of 2 million American troops sent to France.

During the course of the war at least 14 different U-boats operated in the area. The U-8 and U-57 both sank 5 ships each, U-34 sank 6 whilst UB-40 and U-81 scored 11 each. The top score was registered by U-75 with 21 vessels destroyed. Leutenant Wilcke and his crew in the U-37 were lost when they were rammed and sunk by an armed trawler off Fécamp on 31st March 1915. This occurred just after the sinking of the **Emma,**

1,617 tons on a voyage from Dunkirk to Bordeaux in ballast. The U-8 was caught in an explosive anti-submarine net near Dover after sinking 5 ships off Beachy Head in February 1915. The U-34 which sunk the **Meda,** 2,513 tons carrying oranges on 23 March 1915 was herself sunk later in a strange confrontation in the north Russian waters of the White Sea, when under the command of Kapitan-Leutenant Schmitd. The U-boat was attacking a merchant ship by shellfire when an explosion on the merchantman blew a lorry off the deck which landed on the conning tower of the U-boat sending her to the bottom.

Happier times were recalled for a brief moment in March 1915 when one night a number of lights appeared at sea which gradually came nearer to the Pier. In the morning a fleet of small ships were seen at anchor with

SS Ushala and U-121 stranded under Bailey's Brow (Dr S J Surtees)

some moored at the Pier. A flotilla of 12 minesweepers had put in for supplies. The ships were in fact paddle steamers some of which had plied from the Pier giving holidaymakers prc-war pleasure trips. The **Brighton Queen,** the **Westward Ho** and the **Glen Avon** were recognised as being part of the P & A Campbell White Funnel Fleet. Before civic hospitality could be afforded the next day the ships had departed.

For a number of years two wrecks were stranded on the rocks below the cliffs to the west of Birling Gap but neither were directly the result of combat. The **Usahla** an Italian vessel of 3,000 tons, was wrecked in November 1916. In April 1919 six U-boats under tow bound for Brest as part of the reparations to France broke from their towing vessels in bad weather, one the U-118, came ashore by the Queens Hotel at Hastings whilst another U-130, sank five miles south of Beachy Head. The U-121 was stranded alongside the Usahla below Bailey's Brow, both were later broken up for scrap.

The effect of U-boat activity touched the town in other ways. One of Eastbourne's first naval casualties was ordinary seaman Jack Hancock of 68 Firle Road who was lost when the U-9 torpedoed and sank the cruiser **HMS Hawke** on 15th October 1914 in the North Sea off the Firth of Forth. There were just 21 survivors seaman Hancock was not amongst them. The U-9 had, three weeks earlier, been responsible for the sinking of the three ships noted in the second paragraph of this chapter. As suddenly as the onslaught on shipping started so the reports ceased. More effective patrolling together with the use of airships drove some of the U-boats elsewhere. Censorship became tighter and no longer would local newspapers be able to report the successes of the "Pirates" as the submariners were called. Mine laying submarines began to spread their deadly cargoes and the sinkings continued. Further ranging submarines enabled ocean going vessels in the Atlantic to be targeted, this resulting in severe food shortages in Britain, apparent in the Eastbourne shops from 1917 onwards.

11. POLEGATE ROYAL NAVAL AIRSHIP STATION

The British flying services had developed rapidly around the turn of the century. The Royal Engineers (REs) had pioneered the use of balloons for observation purposes. An air battalion of the REs had been formed at Farnborough Hants in 1911 with two airships. The same year the Admiralty had formed a flying training school for airplane pilots at Eastchurch Kent. Both were absorbed into the Royal Flying Corps when it was formed in 1912. At the same time a chain of defensive air stations was set up along the East Coast. The Admiralty regained control of naval aviation just before the outbreak of war in August 1914 with the formation of the Royal Naval Air Service (RNAS). The two flying services continued until April 1918 when both were amalgamated to form the Royal Air Force.

RANS Polegate Coppice Avenue with A22 top rt *(FAA Museum)*

Following the shipping losses to the German U-boats in the North Sea and the Channel, the Admiralty decided to institute air patrols using airships. A 142 acre meadowland site to the south of Polegate was selected in early 1915. It had good road and railway access and was sheltered from the prevailing wind. The area was in the parish of Willingdon stretching from the British Queen to Willingdon (Polegate) Mill and westward to Wannock and the Downs. According to service

SS Z30 cruises by airsheds and windshields at Polegate

protocol, its name was decided by the nearest railway station, Polegate. It was a difficult site for the builders, waterlogged and defying most attempts to drain it. William Arroll and Company, (of Forth Bridge fame) was given the task of constructing the first airship shed which was to be 322 feet long by 70 feet wide and 50 feet high. The building was constructed of bolted wooden trusses supporting corrugated iron sheeting on concrete foundations and flooring.

The station was commissioned on 6th July 1915. The officers were housed in two thatched cottages at Wannock, one remains to this day, whilst the ratings were dispersed to billets in Polegate, Wannock and Willingdon. By the end of 1915, three SS Submarine scout airships were operational carrying out daily patrols along the Sussex coast under the control of the Dover Command.

Early in 1916 a second airship shed of similar size was constructed and a series of accommodation wooden huts were erected close to the A22 road in the area now occupied by Willingdon Court and Thurrock Close. The main entrance to the station was by Coppice Avenue where the Guard Room and administration blocks were located. Close to the present day Willingdon Library was the motor transport depot. This was another corrugated iron structure which together with an attendant wooden hut remained until 1997 as a light engineering works. The new buildings enabled the 14 officers and 137 ratings to move on to the site. The wireless station with dangerously tall masts for airships was located between the Mill and Broad Road away from the main flying area. Also in this vicinity were the bomb and fuse stores.

All the airships to fly from Polegate were of the non-rigid type without an internal framework. Their shape was maintained by hydrogen and hot air contained within the balloon fabric. The first type of airship, the Sea Scout, flown from Polegate, was a primitive combination of an aeroplane fuselage attached to a balloon by wire cables. The balloon contained two internal balloonets filled with inflammable lighter-than-air hydrogen gas. The rest of the main balloon was filled with hot air from the engine of the aeroplane fuselage slung beneath. The first airships used a BE 2C aeroplane minus wings and rudder. The engine was a Renault 75-horse power with 8 cylinders designed to give an aeroplane a speed of 75 mph. With the bulk of the airship's balloon above, only half the designed airspeed could be achieved, this leading to over-heating and frequent breakdowns. These often occurred whilst on patrol over the sea and crews became adept at effecting repairs and restarting the engine whilst gripping struts with their knees. The airship was 145 feet long and had a diameter of 28 feet, its total capacity amounted to 60,000 cubic feet. The nose of the balloon was stiffened with canes.

The Downs form a backdrop for a ground crew at work

The front cockpit would be occupied by the observer who also operated the wireless, the pilot sat in the rear cockpit. The war equipment consisted of one 120-pound bomb or sixteen 20-pound bombs. Four to six handling ropes were provided. The operational height would be about 1,000 feet.

A much larger type of airship next appeared on the scene the Coastal Class (C) with an envelope length of 195 feet and diameter of 37 feet. It had a purpose built car with two skids instead of landing wheels and was engined with two 150hp Sunbeam engines, one in front tractor fashion the other a pusher in the rear giving a maximum speed of 45 mph. The envelope capacity was 170,000 cu ft with the car being 34 feet long. It could take up to five crew members, Pilot, Coxswain, Observer, Wireless operator and Mechanic. It was armed with two Lewis guns and a mixed load of bombs totalling 400 pounds. With its size and overall weight of four tons it was an awkward and difficult airship to manhandle and after its arrival at Polegate the ground crews felt "saddled with it". Much pleasure was expressed when one of the Coastal class C40 was painted black and transferred to the western front in France for clandestine operations. Some of the class were sold to the Italian Air force and eventually Polegate was able to take delivery of the Zero (Z) class of airships.

Control car of a Zero airship with sandbag ballast evident

The Z class was to form the backbone of the station's anti-submarine patrols for the rest of the war. Seventy-six of the Z class were built with 12 serving at Polegate. The craft was 143 feet long, 47 feet high and 39 feet wide equipped with a Rolls Royce 75hp water cooled Hawk engine giving a top speed of 45 mph. Apart from the improved performance and ease of ground handling the crew comfort had been improved. In naval fashion the wooden crew car had become boat shaped complete with keel. The wireless operator occupied the forward position and acted as the Lewis gunner. The pilot sat in the middle cockpit with flight and valving controls whilst the engineer sat in the rear compartment.

Operationally Polegate was one of eleven such stations around the British coast stretching from Anglesey via Mullion in Cornwall, Warsash near Southampton, Capel near Folkestone and the East coast, Howden in Yorkshire, to Arbroath in Scotland. Polegate was under the command of Dover until July 1917 when it was transferred to the Portsmouth command. From early 1918 it had satellite mooring out stations at Slindon near Horsham and Upton at the head of Poole Harbour. About the same time a Wing Headquarters with its own wireless telegraphy station was established on the road from Westham to Hankham. This station had four wooden box aerials 70 feet tall, six huts and a sentry box suggesting a complement of about a dozen men. Another outpost was the meteorological station on Beachy Head opposite the old Racecourse stand near Bullock Down Farm. The "Met" office consisted of one hut 41 feet by 10 feet with smaller ancillary buildings.

The Polegate station was the most active of all of the airship stations. Its patrol area increased from 1,500 square miles in 1916 to 4,500 in 1918 with 8,140 hours flown in 1918 putting it ahead of all the other stations. On 11th August 1918, SS Z39 made a record flight of 51 hours returning with just one gallon of fuel on board, the engine having run continuously throughout the patrol. During all this activity no ship was lost in the area due to submarine attack whilst under airship escort. The patrol limits stretched from Dungeness to Portland Bill. Flying at patrol height off Brighton on 18th April 1918, the SS Z30 sighted a swirl of water with an oil slick thought to be a U-boat track. A bomb was dropped into the slick which brought up a large patch of oil, no further movements were detected in the water. Earlier, in December 1915 the local newspapers reported that Lieutenant Viney, who had trained at Eastbourne, had attacked and sunk a submarine off Middlekerke, Belgium. Despite a number of attacks against suspected submarines, German records examined after the war failed to show any losses which might have been attributed to airships. Much patrolling was carried out in conjunction with Short 184 floatplanes operating from the seaplane base on the eastern side of Newhaven harbour.

The station made a major contribution to the safety of balloon crews when in 1916 successful trials were made of a parachute. Tethered hydrogen filled balloons were used to a considerable extent on the western front as observation platforms for artillery. They would be a prime target for opposing aircraft and anti-aircraft guns. As the balloons would catch fire easily this left the observer with no chance of survival. The Calthrop Guardian Angel parachute was designed as a static parachute fixed to the balloon basket and activated by a pull on the ripcord when the observer jumped for his life. Sir Bryan Leighton, a Colonel of the Westmorland and Cumberland Yeomanry, who had passed through the Upavon flying school in 1914 volunteered, at the age of 48, to make the test jumps which took place on 5th August 1916. As a preliminary, dummy tests were made with weights of 12 stone from heights of 200 and 1,000 feet. The tests were satisfactory and Sir Bryan's jump from 900 feet was entirely successful. It is of interest that the airship from which he jumped was SS13, thus superstition played no part in the test. Although parachutes were introduced for balloonists they were not issued to airship crews and did not become mandatory for RAF aircrew until 1926.

Maintenance of the station and the airships continued to improve. Concrete roads were laid which followed the present day line of Coppice Avenue to Broad Road and from there along to Wannock Avenue. A parade ground complete with naval style flag staff was laid out near Tott Yew Road and the recreation ground. A Silicol Hydrogen gas generation plant with nine gasholders was installed alongside the hangars. With such a dangerously explosive gas all servicing involving electrical equipment, such as wireless sets and batteries, had to be carried out with extreme care. Soldering irons were heated outside the hangers and rushed in by apprentices to the artificers working on the airship cars or rigging. In the early days it took ground crews five days to re-rig and inflate an airship. By 1918 this could be achieved in ten hours. One of the daily tasks was the purity check on the hydrogen content of the inner balloonets.

The station contributed to the war time increase of road traffic and accidents. A collision at Polegate Cross Roads made news in September 1915 when a RANS lorry and a car driven by a Mr Bucke of London were in collision. Both vehicles were badly damaged but there were no serious injuries. Again in May 1918 a motor van belonging to the RANS returning to Polegate from Eastbourne Station hit a tree in Upperton Road and overturned. The van was badly damaged but no injuries were sustained.

By September 1917 six Z class ships were operational when Admiral Sir Stanley Collville, C in C Portsmouth, made a tour of inspection. He took a short test flight in one of the airships and whilst aloft a freshening wind caused an immediate recall signal to be made. Soon three airships were struggling to get moored. All ended well, the Admiral's airship managed to land safely and the C in C now had firsthand operational knowledge.

On one occasion an airship was due to land at Polegate when its engine failed, a northeasterly wind took charge and the airship ascended to 4,000 feet and finally came down near Rouen in France. It was repaired and returned under its own power to base the next day. A carrier pigeon on board had been released over Rouen and returned to Polegate before the airship. On another occasion an airship patrolling from the outstation at Upton made a forced landing near Lewes in a thunderstorm. SS Z30 made a forced landing at Beachy Head in March 1917. In April 1917, SS 13 sustained engine failure 30 miles south of Beachy Head but was rescued by a destroyer, which securing the trail rope from the airship, towed her back to Newhaven. In June of the same year a further loss occurred when SS Z16 came down in a forced landing.

The Willingdon Hill Farm Accident

Five airships set out on patrol in the morning of 20th December 1917. The weather was sunny but hazy, when suddenly at 3.00 pm a thick black fog came down. The airships that were recalled could be heard above at the base but could not be seen. Standing orders for such conditions were to make for open country and this the pilots did. SS Z6 landed near Little Horsted south of Uckfield. Arthur Fordham, a child at the time at Church Farm, recalled going with an older brother to fetch cows in for milking, when in thick fog they heard voices from above enquiring as to the location, the older brother plucked up courage to reply. A rope with a grapnel came down which they tied to a tree.

Three men came down the rope and asked to be directed to the nearest house which was Little Horsted Manor and it was here that Lieutenant J Havers and his crew were made comfortable until they and their deflated ship could be collected by a ground crew from Polegate.

HORSTED PLACE.

Little Horsted near Uckfield SS Z6 landed here

Airships SS Z9 and 10 landed at Hill Farm Willingdon which stands near the 636 feet benchmark and moored safely. SS Z7 and 19 landed near the Coast Guard Station at Beachy Head. By now snow had now fallen. At 8.00 pm an east wind sprang up clearing the fog from the air station but at the same time causing the airships at Beachy Head to drag on their moorings. With the possibility of a gale developing the moored out ships were recalled to Polegate. SSZ7 and 19 from Beachy Head were the first to leave. Over Hill Farm Aldis lights used to illuminate SSZ 9 and 10 were seen by the pilots of the two airships from Beachy Head and mistaken for Polegate's landing lights.

Lieutenant Swallow pilot of SS Z7 descended striking SS Z10 and ripping open the balloon, Lt. Swallow immediately accelerated but in so doing, flames from his engine's exhaust ignited the escaping hydrogen from SS Z10, both ships being engulfed in the flames. Lt Swallow was killed instantly, his engineer and wireless operator were both severely injured. All three were found alongside the airship's car, Air Mechanic Robinson and Boy Mechanic Steere were unable to move the men so instead they carried away the red hot bombs from the bomb racks to a safe distance. As Lieutenant Watson dashed to the blazing wreckage believing that the crew was still trapped, both 65 lb bombs exploded blowing off his right arm.

Remains at Hill Farm 21-12-17

The injured men were taken into Hill Farm Cottages and tended. One of the farm workers son's was sent with a message asking for help to the nearest telephone which was at the "Eight Bells", Jevington. The rescue party led by Station Medical Officer Surgeon-Captain Grahame-Robertson toiled up the Butts Brow track, the wounded were taken to the Central Military Hospital in Church Street (latterly St Mary's

Hospital) where they all eventually recovered. Both A/M Robinson and B/M Steere received the Albert Medal in Gold, Lieutenant Watson was awarded the Albert Medal in Bronze. Little can be found today of Hill Farm apart from some flint walling and in a copse the foundations of the Farm cottages where the wounded were tended. Flight Sub Lieutenant R Swallow who came from Gravesend is buried in Ocklynge Cemetery, his grave looking towards Willingdon Hill where he died. The Albert Medal in Gold award to Boy Mechanic Steere was unique to the RNAS, it appeared in a medal catalogue in 1979 valued at £4,100.

As the war progressed an acute manpower shortage made itself felt. This led to the creation of the women's auxiliary services. Members of the Women's Royal Naval Auxiliary Corps (Wrens) were drafted into Polegate under a Chief Wren. The 54 women performed invaluable tasks as cooks, clerks, drivers, fabric workers and telegraphists. It was deemed unsuitable for the women to live on the station so accommodation was found for them in a large Victorian detached house standing in its own grounds in Willingdon Church Street. Shortlands as it was then known still stands today and is now Haystoun House. It was used as a local authority care home and it has recently been extended and converted into private flats.

The station reflected the usual complement of service departments and those activities of a social kind. Local residents were persuaded to help with the gardens. A monthly journal known as "The Ripping Panel" started at the end of 1917, and a closedown souvenir booklet provides an insight into station life. Sports teams flourished, a brass band with a string section for dances and concerts would have had popular appeal.

The inevitable camp concert party would provide light relief and an opportunity to ridicule authority. The YMCA hut from the now redundant tented camp at Whitbread Hollow was moved to Polegate at Admiralty expense in 1917.

Camp cinema shows were also popular. Sports days were held in the summers of 1917 and 1918 with an estimated attendance of 2,000 visitors.

A happy note was struck on 10th July 1918 with a report in the Eastbourne Gazette of a wedding at St Mary's Parish Church, Willingdon, between Colonel A D Cunningham and Miss H Coles of Milton Road. After the ceremony an airship from the station hovered over the Church and dropped a boot as a good luck symbol.

The first Commanding Officer was Lieutenant Lock, Major J B Cole Hamilton was the CO when the station closed. By 1918 the complement had risen to 37 officers and 264 men. During the life of the station ten of the other ranks gained commissions and 17 officers and men were decorated for bravery and service. Thirteen officers and men were mentioned in dispatches. The Roll of Honour lists four officers and ten other ranks who served at the station and who died on active service. These include two who died from influenza during the 1918 pandemic and one United States Navy ensign undergoing training at Polegate.

With the Armistice, flying was cut drastically and with its purpose served the station closed in April 1919 having lived up to its motto "Semper Paratus - Always Prepared". The local MP, Mr Rupert Gwynne, asked a question in the House in November 1919 about the current status of the station. In reply he was informed that it was being used for the storage and disposal of surplus airships and materials. There were two officers and 22 other ranks on site. All 15 Women's RAF members had been demobilised. Auctioneers notices appeared in July 1921 when Messrs Lake and Company, of Bolton Road, Eastbourne advertised a 3-day sale commencing 3rd August. The two enormous hangars were listed with smaller wooden huts and officers sleeping quarters in all comprising 19 rooms. Bathrooms, a billiards' room, kitchens and boiler houses complete with boilers. A water tower, gasometer, latrines, flagstaff and wireless masts also featured. A veritable treasure trove of tools, fittings, electrical equipment, building supplies, paints, oils, aircraft dope were included. A magic lantern, a Ross telescope, wireless transmitting and receiving sets were amongst the more unusual items to be offered. Surprisingly, a complete light railway also came under the hammer presumably used in construction of roads and buildings in the early days of the base.

Today some relics survive. Many of the concrete mooring blocks with the iron rings known as tethers lurk in gardens of Lower Willingdon, some disguised as rockeries and a full set of five lie in woodland at Donkey Hollow. The lawn of the Vicarage in Broad Road dries in square brown patches in hot summers due to concrete remains concealed just below the surface. Developers after the Second World War had to use explosives to remove some of the more difficult concrete obstructions.

A house in Wannock Lane is built on a plinth of bricks recovered from buildings demolished on the site. The house also boasts a garden shed which the owner's father bought and moved on rollers with the aid of a horse from its original site where it was used as a guardhouse. Mornings Mill Farm also has some of the steelwork to support farm bridges over culverts. The most significant reminder of the airship station, a corrugated iron and concrete motor transport workshop, survived until 1995 when it was claimed by bungalow development. The structure, having been used for many years by Bird's Engineering, stood next door to Willingdon Library in Coppice Avenue.

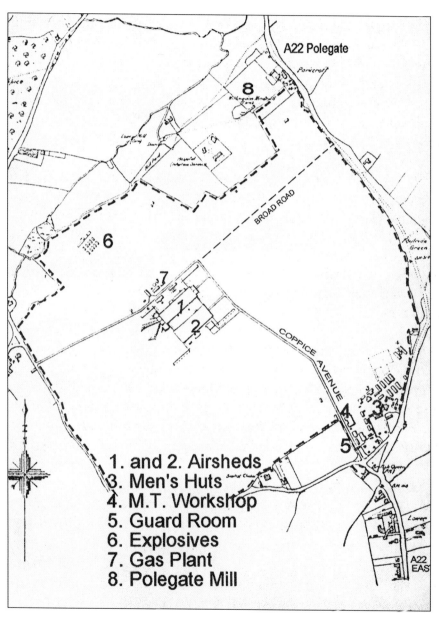

1. and 2. Airsheds
3. Men's Huts
4. M.T. Workshop
5. Guard Room
6. Explosives
7. Gas Plant
8. Polegate Mill

Plan of Polegate RANS Station 1918 amended (Crown Copyright)

12. ROYAL NAVAL FLYING SCHOOL

Seaplane station at the Crumbles

On 1st December 1911 the Eastbourne Flying School opened on a 50 acre site on Willingdon Levels to the west of St Anthony's Hill. The initiative for the school came from Mr Frederick Bernard Fowler who taught himself to fly before taking his certificate on 16th January 1912. Fowler teamed up with another local aviation pioneer, Frank Hucks in 1913 and on 13th of February they formed the Eastbourne Aviation Company.

A site on the Crumbles was leased from Lord Willingdon and a factory to build seaplanes was erected. A slipway to the high tide level and a turntable was installed to facilitate launching. The factory was located near today's Sovereign Centre. In 1913 the Admiralty began to take an interest in the venture and leased a shed on the St Anthony's Hill site and subsidised the construction of two hangars at the Crumbles.

When the war commenced in August 1914, private flying was suspended. The Crumbles site was used as a refuelling and servicing station for patrolling floatplanes. It was undoubtedly conveniently situated between Capel at Folkestone in the east and Newhaven in the west where similar stations were located. The hangars at the Crumbles were converted into an aircraft factory.

In September 1914 St Anthony's was requisitioned by the Admiralty as a flying training school for probationary Sub-Lieutenants under Squadron Commander P A Shepherd. Mr Fowler soon became part of the service establishment with the commissioned rank of temporary Flight Lieutenant and successive promotions followed to Major in 1918, an unusual rank in the newly fledged Royal Air Force. Frank Huck joined the Navy's Engineering branch reaching the rank of Engineer Lieutenant Commander.

By October 1915, Eastbourne had become a vital training centre for pilots. A mixed bag of aeroplanes constituted the establishment, seven Bleriot Monoplanes, three Caudron G IIIs, seven Curtis JN3s, four Grahame White Xvs, six Maurice Farmans, two White and Thompson "Bognor Bloaters" a Bristol TB8 and a BE2c. For a few weeks in the autumn of 1916 a Wright 840 Landplane bomber was used for training until it was written off in a crash. By mid-1916 Maurice Farman's and Curtis JN4A "Jennys" were being used.

In order to accommodate the large and varied number of aircraft additional hangar space was required. Seventeen Bessaneau hangars were erected. These consisted of a light steel framework with a stout canvas cover, the tent flap like doors were secured with ropes and toggles and in nautical style rope ladders were fitted to the hangar fronts to enable ratings to climb up to secure the upper toggles. The hangars were 90

Bessaneau Hangar

feet long by 13 feet high and had a span of 64 feet. They would comfortably house six of the training planes then in use. One row of the hangars fronted the line of the present day Leeds Avenue whilst a double row was located at right angles to Lottbridge Drove in what is now Birch Road.

In order to secure adequate take off and landing distances the Eastbourne Aviation Company had boarded over the ditches which intersect the wet meadows, a feature of the Levels. However it was felt that more space was needed and accordingly the total area under service control was extended to cover an area five times that of the original landing field.

RNAS "A" Flight 1917 pose by a Bessaneau hangar *(FAA Museum)*

The extended area stretched from the Birdseye roundabout along St Anthony's Avenue to the Langney roundabout, Langney Rise to the eastern end of Sevenoaks Road returning along the route of the Willingdon Sewer to Lottbridge Drove at Birch Road. In April 1917, due to this expansion of the aerodrome the public was excluded from Lottbridge Drove under the Defence of the Realm Act. Exceptions were made for dustcarts, airfield traffic and allotment holders with passes.

The original entrance to the aerodrome was from Seaville Drive which lines up with the Guardhouse, now occupied by a private resident and accessible only from Leeds Avenue. In order to make life easier both on the ground and in the air the Eastbourne Council considered and granted two requests from the station commander. In January 1918 the Council agreed to remove two sewer-ventilating columns in Lottbridge Drove which were considered to be a hazard to flying. A request in March 1918 to remove three trees in Seaside for a new entrance to the station was reduced to permission to remove two. In January 1918 the Council was asked to agree to the Hampden Park Playing fields being used for practice take offs and landings, when not required for matches.

Activity at the station was such that the electricity power supply became overloaded. In July 1915 it became necessary to install a new high pressure cable and substation which the Admiralty agreed to pay for. It was this payment which may have contributed to a delay in paying for electricity consumed. The council finally reported that the Admiralty had paid up by December 1917. The air station, a sub-station to Cranwell, closed temporarily on 9th November 1916 on transfer of the station activities to Vendóme in France. It re-opened on 1st May 1917. On creation of the Royal Air Force on 1st March 1918 it became the home of No 206 Training Depot Squadron (TDS) and then No 50 TDS on 15th July 1918, finally closing early in 1919.

The Eastbourne Aviation Company's works at the Crumbles soon became an important constructor of aircraft for the RNAS and the RFC. Completed planes would be flown off Manser's track (Royal Parade) on the south east side of the Gilbert Recreation Ground (Princes Park) for the one mile flight to the RNAS station at St Anthony's Hill before delivery to other RNAS and RFC stations elsewhere.

Flying was in its infancy in 1914 just 11 years having elapsed since the Wright brothers' first flight. Aviation was an inexact science which, coupled with elementary aeroplanes, led unfortunately to a number of accidents to aircraft and pilots of the flying training school. The construction of the planes was, by today's standards, flimsy. The wings, fuselage and control surfaces were made of a wooden framework, this was usually spruce. Cross wires were used to brace the framework. It would be glued, pinned and jointed in the manner of coachbuilding. A fabric cover, heavy linen or canvas stretched tight over the framing would be sewn into position. The surfaces would then be painted with several coats of a type of varnish known as dope. The engine, usually air cooled, would be the most robust part of the plane giving a speed of

Maurice Farnham Longhorn 1917

around 70 mph. The control surfaces would be operated manually by wires led over pulley wheels to the rudder and elevators. The fragile planes afforded little protection to the pilots in accidents. Pilots flew without parachutes.

Accidents and Fatalities

2nd June 1915 Following engine trouble Lieutenant L C Keble crash landed near some houses receiving non-fatal injuries. He was taken to Kempston Auxiliary Red Cross Hospital, Blackwater Road, for treatment.

13th June 1915 Two BEc2 planes recently completed at the Crumbles works were due for delivery to St Anthony's Hill. The first made the short journey uneventfully, the second piloted by Sub-Lieutenant Arthur Gelston Shepherd aged 20, had experienced engine faltering during pre-take off warm up, eventually he took off, rose in the air, circled the works and appeared to suffer engine misfires. The plane appeared not to gain power and height and circled over the sea in an attempt to land. It failed to gain the beach coming down in shallow water about 200 yards out. Rescuers swam out and a boat was summoned but the pilot was found to be trapped under water in the upside down wreckage by bracing wires. At the inquest the Coroner, Mr Vere Benson noted that it was his first inquest into an aviator's death. He was buried at Wooton Berks.

21st July 1915 A man in a train at Hampden Park about 5.30 pm saw a plane make a forced landing on the levels. He made his way to the scene and with a number of other helpers held down the tail of the plane whilst the pilot revved up the engine. On the signal to let go the plane raced forward and slewed to one side. It nose dived into a ditch and turned over. The pilot and observer were both shaken but unhurt, the plane was badly damaged.

15th January 1916 An aeroplane crashed in Alderman Martin's brickyard east of Hampden Park station. Arkwright Road off Willingdon Drove is the nearest identifiable spot. At the inquest it was reported that on take off the plane was in good order. Witnesses on the ground heard shouted commands from the pilot in charge to the pupil. Three separate switch offs and restarts of the engine were called for, on the last command the plane nose-dived into the ground. An examination of the wreckage suggested that some of the flight surface control wires had come off pulley wires causing a loss of control of the plane. Flight-Sub-Lieutenant Duke, aged 19, RNAS, of Toronto, Canada and Warrant Officer Percival Victor Fraser, of Rockhampton, Queensland, Australia are buried side by side at Ocklynge in a privately marked grave.

10th March 1917 Lieutenant Denys Fowler died at St Anthony's when his aircraft crashed. The plane was seen to make a flat turn without banking it nose-dived and crashed upside down, petrol from the ruptured fuel tank was ignited by sparks from the magneto. He was buried at Rottingdean.

Boarded runways and wrecked Bognor "Bloaters"

16th June 1917 A squadron of airplanes left an airfield in Wiltshire at 1.15 pm for Eastbourne stopping twice on the way to refuel before arriving over St Anthony's Hill at 5.30 pm. In one of the planes were Lieutenants Herd and Newton, the latter having had 20 hours' flying experience. A landing attempt failed with an overshoot of the runway, another circuit of the landing ground was attempted but the plane nose-dived from 80 feet. Fire broke out in the wreckage, the resultant fireball reaching 100 feet. Lieutenant Henry Irvine Newton who had been flying the plane managed to escape but Lieutenant Rupert Holmes Herd aged 25, Australian Flying Corps, of Ringwood, Victoria, Australia was trapped and died. He is buried in Ocklynge Cemetery. The bearer and firing party for the funeral came from the Cavalry Command Depot.

23rd January 1918 A plane was seen to crash in the Crumbles pond, now Princes Park Lake. The pilot was rescued by civilians. A letter of thanks to the rescuers from Squadron Commander F Fowler appeared in the

BE2c 8-4-16 built by EAC Co.

Eastbourne Chronicle. The accident took place on a Sunday and the rescuers had plunged in their best clothes into two feet of mud and water to assist the pilot.

30th January 1918 An airman of the United States Air Corps, Officer Cadet Roy O Garber aged 26, on a flight from Shoreham to Eastbourne was seen to circle over the aerodrome and make a tight right hand turn. The plane stalled at 150 feet and nose dived into the gas works yard (Finmere Road) the pilot was taken to the Central Military Hospital in Church Street, where he died from his injuries. He was buried in

Ocklynge but after the war was re-buried in the United States section of Brookwood Cemetery, Surrey.

20th March 1918 Probationary Flying Officer Brown was sitting in a machine waiting to take off in hazy weather conditions. A collision occurred with another plane piloted by Probationary Flying Officer John Phillip aged 18 who had only been flying since 10th February. F. O. Phillip descended from 1,000 feet and having a restricted view through the propeller failed to see the stationary aircraft. He sustained multiple injuries and his remains were returned to his home town, Chingford, for burial.

12th June 1918 A young aviator William Stanley Pullen lost his life after 20 hours flying practice. He took off at 8.20 am from St Anthony's to practise landings, two were successfully made. On the third attempt his plane stalled. He crashed into the ground from a height of 50 feet near the Aylesbury Dairy (Aylesbury Avenue). His home was in Slough.

19th June 1918 A farmworker, Mr F W Elstone of Hamlands Farm, was cutting grass with a horse-drawn mowing machine at the aerodrome. At the same time a Brazilian pilot undergoing instruction flew low over the mowing machine startling the horses. It is unclear whether the plane hit the farmworker but he succumbed to injuries received in the impact or from the machinery. No explanation was offered at the inquest as to effect of the collision on the plane. The pilot, Chauro Arango, with 17 hours' flying experience 9 of these being solo, hobbled in to the Coroner's Court on sticks, the inference being made that the plane came down heavily and he too was injured. Later in March 1919 a successful claim under the Workmen's Compensation Act was made by Mrs Elstone who was left with children to support. She received £289 compensation, her husband had earned £1:14 shillings per week as a farm labourer.

22nd August 1918 Flight Lieutenant Robert Kirkwood Calloway, aged 23, on his first solo flight misjudged a turn, the plane went to a spin and crashed. He died in the Central Military Hospital Church Street.

28th August 1918 Lieutenant Charles Albert Manzetti from Clapham, London, aged, 25 had made two take offs and landings. On the third ascent the pilot circled and crashed. He is buried in Ocklynge.

Sopwith Pup 50th Training Depot Squadron

4th September 1918 Flight Cadet Phillip George Winchester, aged 24, of the 63rd Training Squadron RAF was flying at 1,000 feet when part of the wing fabric became detached, the wing collapsed causing the plane to crash. His home was in Winchelsea Road and he had formerly served in France in a regiment of the King Edward's Horse. He is buried in Ocklynge Cemetery.

The Guardroom at Leeds Avenue 1999

5th September 1918 A practice formation flight at 1,000 feet came to grief with a mid-air collision. The accident claimed the lives of two pilots when Lieutenant Reginald Horace Sanders aged 24, whose parents lived at Hampden Park, collided with a Brazilian Naval trainee pilot, Lieutenant Eugenio de Silva Possolo. The latter is buried in a privately marked grave in Ocklynge. An elaborate headstone has unfortunately been vandalised in recent years.

5th September 1918 Lieutenant William Barnett aged 27 died whilst on his third solo flight. The plane was just 80 feet up when the pilot lost control of the plane. He crashed after attempting a third loop too close to the ground. A witness from Hailsham reported that he had seen the plane crash into woodland.

Steel hangars survived until the 1987 hurricane

20th November 1918 Private Hugh Hancock Hamill 321 Squadron United States Army Air Corps, died in the Central Military Hospital Church Street from gas gangrene.

He had suffered a leg injury on 10th November, on the eve of the Armistice. An accident occurred during the manual swinging of an aircraft's propeller, the normal method for an engine start, when a hot engine fired more quickly than expected. He is buried in Brookwood Cemetery, Surrey.

Six men of the Royal Air Force and one man from the Unites States Air Force died in the Central Military Hospital as a result of the influenza pandemic of 1918.

The trainees were intended on passing out to fly in bomber squadrons on the Western Front in France. Pilots from Australia, Canada, Brazil and the United States were taught alongside those from England. The United States declared war on Germany in April 1917 and Brazil in October the same year.

An index of activity can be gauged by the closing establishment in 1918

Personnel

Officers	51
Officers under Instruction	120
NCOs under Instruction	60
Staff Warrant Officers and NCOs	72
Rank and File	320
Forewomen	7
Women (Technical)	155
Women (Household)	54
Total	839

Transport

Touring Cars	1
Light Cars	10
Heavy Tenders	8
Motor Cycles	8
Sidecars	8
Trailers	5
Total	36

Aeroplanes

Camels	38
Avros	38
Total	76

The aerodrome extended to 242 acres measuring 2,000 by 1,000 yards and the 35 station buildings covered 10 acres. Two large sheds are listed as being 179 feet by 59 feet and 59 by 69 feet and these remained on site until the hurricane of 1987. They sustained damage which necessitated their demolition. Previously they had been used for storing vintage buses. An earlier existence had been as a furniture repository for Wenham's, a well known Auctioneers and Removals firm, who owned much of the land at St Anthony's Hill.

A Regimental institute and stores were listed, as were seven huts for the men as dormitories. Lecture huts, a compass platform, four workshops, offices, latrines, first aid hut, motor transport and gunnery workshops completed the schedule. Officers and other ranks were accommodated in rented buildings in the town and without doubt the women would have been accommodated off base.

Transport between the aerodrome and the town would be by motor tender which would call at Officers Messes at South Lynn, Mill Road and Eversley Court in St Annes Road. St Vincent's in Carlisle Road and Redmont at the corner of Trinity Place and Compton Street were also used for accommodation, Holmbury 11, Upper Avenue also housed a women's RAF hostel. The Officers' Mess at South Lynn made the local headlines on 26th February 1919 when the Eastbourne Fire Brigade attended to put out fires which started under the main staircase. Not to be out done a fire broke out in the bar at Eversley Court affecting two upper rooms. The airmen escaped down ropes made of knotted sheets.

A wedding took place on 25th October 1918 at the Central Methodist Church between Lieutenant Rundle-Woolcock and a WAAF, a member of the Women's Auxiliary Air Force stationed at the base, Miss Grace Simms. This made local headlines. After the ceremony fellow officers performed aerobatic stunts over the church and flew over the town dropping messages of goodwill. Later they provided an air escort to the train on which the honeymoon couple travelled from Eastbourne. Major

Henry Lees-Smith was the Station commander in its final days. The Armistice brought a very rapid run down in the activities. On the morning of 11th November 1918 some of the men came into the town and drove up and down Terminus Road in the beflagged tenders shouting and cheering.

In 1920 the Council were dealing with planning applications relating to some of the station buildings. It was concerned that they had been erected, by the Admiralty, without planning permission, and did not comply with building regulations. The huts were still being used as workshops, when an application to convert 6 of them to dwellings, was made. Another request was made to convert aeroplane sheds into an iron foundry and a carpentry workshop. These were all deferred until a satisfactory report on the drainage arrangements was received.

Conversion of the old guard room, which also did not have proper drainage, to a bungalow was given temporary approval which, later was extended to 25 years. It still stands today!

The first auction sale of surplus materials was advertised in June 1919 with land drains, timber and builders materials on offer. In January 1921 the auctioneer advertised more building materials, wooden sleepers and the dismantled Bessaneau hangars. The St Anthony's Hill site was re-licensed to the Eastbourne Aviation Company for flying in 1919 but was cancelled at the company's request at the end of the following year. By 1922 the company was in receivership and eventually the remaining buildings went to other commercial uses. The village of Five Ashes has a chapel which formerly did duty as a hut at the aerodrome.

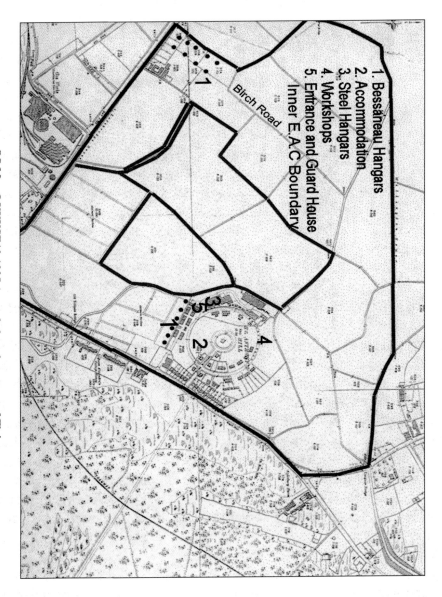

1. Bessaneau Hangars
2. Accommodation
3. Steel Hangars
4. Workshops
5. Entrance and Guard House
   Inner E.A.C Boundary

Birch Road

OS Map LXXXSE10 1925 Amended to show area of Flying

13. THE HOME FRONT

The country went to war with a Liberal Government in power led by Mr Herbert Asquith, in May 1915 a coalition under the same leadership was formed by Conservatives, Liberals and Labour, Mr Lloyd George took over as Prime Minister in December 1916 until the end of the war. Labour withdrew its support for the coalition in 1917. By far the most important contribution which the town made to the war effort was that of man and woman power. The last pre-war census of 1911 recorded 52,542 inhabitants in the town. The numbers had grown about 1,000 per annum since the previous 1901 census. Taking the national population as 42 million with 5.1 million under arms, Eastbourne made a contribution of 7,500 men and women to the services. Traditionally, since the collapse of the feudal system and apart from the press gangs, Great Britain had relied on volunteers for the armed forces in peace and war.

The regular army had sent 120,000 men to France at the outset of the war as the British Expeditionary Force. The regular army of 1914 had a strength of 247,000 men supplemented by a reserve of about 200,000 and the Territorial Army of 260,000. Lord Kitchener, Secretary of State for War's famous appeal for 100,000 men was oversubscribed tenfold. By 1915 the supply of voluntary recruits was dwindling and losses were mounting. It was realised that in addition to providing more recruits it would be necessary to safeguard essential services and ensure that skilled men needed for the production of war materials remained in their jobs.

In July 1915 the National Registration Bill was enacted which required that all men and women between the ages of 15 and 65 should register. Out of this came the so-called Derby Scheme administered by Lord Derby, Under Secretary for War. The basis was that men between the age of 18 and 41 would sign up or attest. They would only be called up as and when needed, dependent on marital status, and importance of their jobs to the war effort. It was planned to take all the unmarried unemployed men first. Attesting of recruits was to be placed in the hands of local tribunals. These were composed of local dignitaries and would include a military representative. The tribunals met weekly from February 1915 until November 1918. The Eastbourne tribunal was composed of the Mayor Alderman Charles O'Brien Harding, Aldermen Edward Duke, Major, Molineaux, and Councillor Bishop. As military representative, Mr M H Beattie, was renowned for overcoming an applicants objection to "Call-up". Mr Beattie was often challenged for not joining up himself, but being over military age was exempt from service. As soon as the age limits were altered he confounded his critics by volunteering for the army, eventually serving in France.

YOUR KING AND COUNTRY NEED YOU!

A CALL TO ARMS!

An addition of 100,000 men to His Majesty's Regular Army is immediately necessary in the present grave National Emergency. Lord Kitchener is confident that this appeal will be at once responded to by all those who have the safety of our Empire at heart.

TERMS OF SERVICE:

General Service for a period of 3 years or until the War is concluded.

Age of Enlistment between 19 and 30.

HOW TO JOIN.

Full information can be obtained at any Post Office in the United Kingdom or at any Military Depot.

GOD SAVE THE KING.

In 1918 cases heard included that of a supervising laundry engineer with nine children, and a Red Cross volunteer of medical grade A, who was given an extension of one month's deferment. His employer was told to pool engineering services with other laundries. Another employee was an 18-year-old carpenter working for the Aviation Company he was given an extension of two months before call-up. A hairdresser was given three months in which to join up whilst a harness maker on Army contracts was excused for a year.

In January 1916 a law was passed transferring all single attested men to the army reserve. This measure failed to bring in enough recruits so in May of that year a new Military Service Act was passed making military service compulsory. Conscription, so long opposed, had now arrived. Lord Derby's Scheme had in Eastbourne identified 2,338 single and 4,286 married men as being eligible for service.

Munitionettes at Lovely's Cavendish Place garage

Women took over many of the tasks hitherto considered a male domain. Mr George White saddled pony proprietor, had to ask for a licence for girls to take charge of the sea front children's rides. Among the cases considered by the tribunals was that of the Corporation electricity works which failed to save its workers from call-up in 1918 despite claiming to be a war industry.

War Weapons

By the spring of 1915 the scandal of the "Shell Shortage" became known through publicity in "The Times" and the "Daily Mail". Due to pre-war economies and bureaucratic red tape in the supply departments of the Army, guns at the front in France had been rationed to a handful of shells per day. A number of the battles were adversely affected by the shell shortage. Eastbourne had only light industrial potential for war production. In April 1915 the municipal bus department was asked by the War Office to release mechanics for the army. Instead the department offered to make munitions if machinists could be obtained. Production commenced in October of Stokes two inch trench mortar bombs. Additional lathes were purchased in December 1915 and November 1916. The total wartime production of mortar bombs amounted to 370,000, in addition 3,530 sea mines, supplied in parts from factories at Stratford and Swindon, were welded together.

Lovely's flamethrower

Mr P Ellison, Manager of the Bus Department, served on the Sussex Board of Management for War Production. Despite the Board's observations on the rural character of the county, small firms made significant contributions to the manufacture of bombs, fuses, and small machined items. Howard's Pneumatic Engineering of Fort Road carried out unspecified work as also did Eastbourne Motors of Commercial Road who asked in May 1915 for additional electricity supplies for war work. Messrs Lovely's Cavendish Place Garage made small parts for Tanks and also pioneered a one million candle power flame thrower which, despite having killed three men on its first test, was used on HMS Vindictive for the Zeebrugge Raid. This was a partially successful attempt to block the harbour used by the German navy as a U-boat base. The boys of Eastbourne College after lessons used the workshops to produce 1,400 phosphor bronze collars, 265 sea mine contacts, 112 shell cases and 450 metal handles. Caffyn's Seaside Garage produced aircraft tail planes and rudders. A SE5a plane shot down at Sanctuary Wood in the Ypres Salient bore a maker's panel proclaiming "Caffyn's Ltd, Engineers and Aircraft Manufacturers Eastbourne". Doubt exists regarding the company's manufacture of complete aircraft, as early records of the company were lost during a bombing raid on 6th May 1943, but a former employee claims that 70 planes were made during the 1914-18 war. In January 1919 the company was advertising the sale of a supply of surplus well-seasoned spruce, an essential component of wooden framed aircraft. Rivalry between Caffyn's and Lovely's Garage spilled over into the entertainment scene when both firms announced morale boosting concert parties. Shows were put on in the Town Hall in aid of the Red Cross by Caffyn's. Lovely's used St Saviour's Church Hall in South Street, and even boasted of its own band.

Cottage industry also had a part to play, when in April 1915, Mrs Stephen Fox, of **Angled**, Bolsover Road, appealed for ladies to help with sewing hessian. Apparently a shortage of sandbags for the troops in the trenches had manifested itself. Patterns for the 33 by 14 inch bags would be provided and it was estimated that an infantry battalion could use up to 2,000 per day. Nationally a production target of a million bags was required.

The Eastbourne Aviation Company

The company had commenced in 1911 as a Flying Training School at St Anthony's Hill under the direction of Frederick B Fowler, a self taught pilot. In 1913 Frank Huck's owner of the Huck's Waterplane Company visited Fowler at Eastbourne and on the 18th February 1913 the two

Production bay at the Eastbourne Aviation Company's Crumbles works

firms were amalgamated as the Eastbourne Aviation Company. The company set up seaplane works at the Crumbles and these were enlarged prior to the war by support from the Royal Naval Air Service.

Orders for aircraft were received from the Admiralty for BE2c's and Maurice Farman biplanes for the RANS. These were followed by orders from the War Office for Avro 504a's and 504k's for the RFC. In addition to the new construction a considerable amount of repair work was undertaken. The new planes were built in batches, the contracts were initially in sixes then in 20s and finally in 50s. Two batches, six of BE2'c with Renault 75hp or RAF 90 hp engines, were followed by two batches of 20 Maurice Farman Shorthorn planes with 80hp Renault engines. To complete the service contracts, four batches of 50 Avro 504 planes of various marks were completed with Gnome 80hp engines, six more had 130hp Clerget engines. The total war production amounted to 252 aircraft.

To sustain this effort considerable use was made of women especially in the fabric departments and in the paint and finishing sections. Other changes included extensions to the works in October 1916, in February and October 1917 and finally in September 1918. Although a stationary oil engine was used to generate electricity, the corporation supply was upgraded in 1914 and a water main was laid across the Gilbert Recreation Ground in December 1916. A council minute records the Electricity Department's steam traction engine being used to recover a RNAS lorry and trailer carrying two aeroplanes from the beach, the road by the Gilbert Recreation Ground having collapsed under the weight. To avoid this problem the Aviation Company secured flying rights over the recreation ground from the corporation in 1917 for the sum of £5, which they exercised for six months. An agreement by the company to pay for road repairs allowed the factory's output of planes to be delivered to St Anthony's Hill by lorry. By 1919 aircraft output was dispatched by train from Eastbourne following the run down of St Anthony's Hill air station. On 21st January two aircraft on the loading dock at Eastbourne railway station were damaged by fire having come into contact with a stovepipe from the parcels' office.

Food and Fuel

Following the outbreak of war, food prices rose steadily increasing by 60%. This affected the working classes to a considerable degree, as significant unemployment ensured that wages remained low. The law of supply and demand operated. As the war progressed the eventual labour shortage allowed wages to rise or "War Bonuses" to be secured. Britain needed to import large quantities of food and raw material by sea to further the war effort. By 1916 German submarines were sinking 300,000 tons of ships each month. This rose dramatically in April 1917 when one million tons were lost. The following month a convoy system of protecting shipping was instituted and with American help, losses were curtailed.

Families would spend under £2 per week on food, fuel and heating which amounted to 75% of income. Prices rose and queues for food became commonplace after the end of 1916 especially in the shops which served the poorer parts of the town. It may be conjectured that the well to do having monthly accounts with tradesmen were catered for without the need for queuing. A local newspaper carried a report in 1917 that the hotels had secured ample supplies of dried fruit for the Christmas trade. Later, limited controlled prices and nationally set standards gave a measure of fairness in the availability of food. In May 1917 a severe shortage of food grains became apparent and this led to the King, George V issuing a Royal Proclamation ordering the utmost economy in their use. The National loaf was of high flour extraction and grey in colour. By January 1918 bakers were asked to dilute flour with mashed potato at a rate of ten pounds of potato to 280 pounds of flour and in May this became compulsory.

Rationing of foodstuffs commenced in October 1917 with sugar and it was not until early the following year that meat, ham, bacon, butter and margarine also went on ration. One third of a pound of meat per person per week was allowed, the controlled prices per pound were silverside

Seaside Road 1918 mainly women and girls left to serve the meagre rations

one shilling and threepence, leg of lamb one shilling and tenpence. In January 1918 Sainsbury's advised customers to register with them as butter rationing was imminent. Each week butchers had to report to the Food Control Committee on the amount of meat sold. They also operated a combined slaughtering and cutting system to save labour, hitherto most butchers had carried out these functions independently. Eleven local butchers were fined in February 1919 for selling meat in excess of coupons. By then the war was over and supplies were becoming more plentiful.

Allotments were much sought after and by 1917 the Council had 241 with 71 applicants on the waiting list. The Compton Estate had

Ration coupons for lard and jam

increased the number of plots from 200 to 500, with the Artisans Dwellings Company providing 40 more. The Eastbourne Gas Company refused a Council request to plough up land for allotments as they wished to secure the hay crop, but compulsion under the Lands Order achieved the required result.

By March 1918 the Duke of Devonshire had created 700 plots and war allotments were located at Gaudick Road, Le Brun Road, Prideaux Road, Ashburnham Road and Pocock's Farm on the west side of King's Drive. Others were to be found at The Goffs in Gildredge Park, Old Town Recreation Ground, at Horsey Bank, Seaside and Lottbridge Drove. Mr Wenham's St Anthony's Estate yielded more land which he had difficulty in reclaiming in 1919. Durley Playing Fields and the Municipal School Playing fields, now the Park Avenue rugby pitch, were also used and cultivated by pupils.

The Council itself cultivated ground at Hampden Park and Roselands. The 1917 potato crop was marred by the weather, the late summer and the autumn being exceptionally wet. Most varieties grown were blighted or attacked by wireworm. There was a countywide shortfall of potatoes, 26,000 tons being grown with 59,000 tons needed. The same bad weather had interfered with General Haig's set piece battle in the Ypres Salient which commenced in July and ended in November in a sea of mud at Passchendale. The next year was more successful with yields of nearly five tons potatoes, 496 dozen lettuce, half a ton of tomatoes, 39 bushels (a bushel was approx 56 pounds) of onions and one acre of turnips and cabbages at Hampden Park. However, 4,000 cabbage and cauliflower plants had been grown at Roselands together with 379 bushels of runner beans. Allotment gardening was not without its problems of vandalism, but those in Old Town were the subject of damage by troops at the Command Depot in Victoria Drive. Colonel Follet, Commandant, ordered the plots to be "Out of Bounds" to troops. It was arranged that the fence would be raised and Military Police supervision increased.

The Council's food production had cost £700 and overall produced a net loss of £7. A notice was posted in the parade room at the Eastbourne Police Station calling for volunteers with experience of ploughing to come forward. However there was no response from the constables. Boys of the Municipal Grammar School Cadet Force from the Technical Institute, Grove Road went to summer harvest camps in 1917-1918 at Sissinghurst Kent

An army of clerks had prepared almost 48,000 Ration books for issue, but over 4,000 had been delayed because of insufficient details of the applicants had been given. Seventeen Blue Boys from Summerdown Camp had helped with the work. The manufacture of ice cream was prohibited from January 1918. Milk deliveries were zoned to save labour and transport. Supplementary rations were allowed for those undertaking heavy work such as furniture porters, machinists, nurses, and laundresses. Medical certificates would allow extra food for specific complaints. No known medical condition required finer milled flour. A ten per cent shortage of cheese occurred so plans were made to convert any surplus milk to cheese. The Food Control Committee authorised the sale "Off ration" of surplus bacon, ham and sausage rather than let it go bad. Allegations of wastage of food at the Army camps led to the Committee making inspections under much protest from the

Commandants, snap visits revealed that the complaints were unfounded. Edible oils were reserved for fish and chip shops and were not available to general catering establishments. Hotels were allowed food for catering but hoarding was a crime. An hotelier from Bolton Road who managed to accumulate 280 pounds of rice was fined £10 or one month in prison.

Food control committee working in the Town Hall 1918

A ray of hope to the less well off appeared in March 1918 when a National Kitchen opened at 103 Seaside Road with the Mayor Alderman Harding being the first customer. Eastbourne's hotels had helped to equip the kitchen. The tariff was modest with soup at one penny, roast beef eightpence, cabbage one penny and rice pudding twopence. The venture was so successful that in September further National Kitchens were proposed for South Street, Seaside and Old Town. By October 1919 the kitchens had closed and the council reported that the equipment was stored in the East Street Cavendish Girls', Cookery Schools. Some items of equipment had been removed to the Pitman Institute, Church Street to provide winter meals for poor children.

Transport

At the outset of the war, transport of goods, passengers and the army was dominated by the horse and the railway. Horse drawn carriages, and cabs were for the well off, working people walked, cycled or perhaps

Corporation solid tyred War subsidy bus at the Pier

used the Corporation buses which served the most built-up areas of the town. As an example the Ocklynge route terminated at Selwyn Road the fringe of northern development. Motorised vehicles were considered noisy and unreliable, war-time demands ushered in advances which by 1918 signalled the end of the horse drawn era. The town had two other companies which provided horse drawn cabs and charabancs and some bus services. These were Messrs Bassett's and Chapman's both had mixed fleets of horsedrawn and petrol driven vehicles. Chapman's lost four petrol vehicles to the army and requested licences to use electric powered vehicles. In 1918 the company fell foul of the regulations when they were caught using petrol for unauthorised journeys, namely pleasure trips! Chapman's commenced a twice weekly London service in February 1917 to the Grosvenor Hotel, Victoria with single fares of ten shillings. The coaches went up on Mondays and Fridays returning on Tuesdays and Saturdays. These vehicles ran on coal gas they were much slower than petrol vehicles but at least they were lawful. Despite war-time restrictions a Brighton based company, Southdown Motor Services, started a short lived twice daily service between the two towns in 1915. There were, of course, objections from the two local bus operators Bassett's and Chapman's. Other problems confronted cab and coach owners. In October 1917 a Horse Foodstuffs rationing order prohibited the feeding of cab horses with cereals and the Council recommended that horse cab licences be withdrawn. The RSPCA asked that licences for Horse Charabancs also be withdrawn because of the shortage of oats. By March 1918 all the licences were withdrawn as horses could not do the work on just hay and roots, by then no oats were available at all. Petrol taxi cab proprietors requested that they be allowed to fit roof trays to support coal gas bags in view of the petrol shortage.

Eastbourne has the distinction of being the first Corporation to operate a municipal motorbus service in the country which commenced in 1903 and provided formidable competition to the private companies. At the outset of the war the department was left with 18 serviceable vehicles after six had been requisitioned by the army. Some obsolete Daimlers were converted into dustcarts.

By December 1914 out of 82 drivers and conductors 39 had joined the services. Male replacements were found but eventually in 1917 conductresses were employed and it was reported that they were "working well".

Restrictions on services were made in 1915 with the sea front service being withdrawn and Carew Road having just six buses a day. All

Chapman's coal gas powered London coach

services in the town ceased at 10.00 pm. Petrol shortages became apparent by mid 1917 causing further curtailment of services, the Commandants of the two large military camps were asked to help with petrol supplies to maintain excursions and station journeys for the troops. In December 1915 the War Department agreed to six new buses being supplied, conditional upon them being available for war service if needed. They were known as "War Subsidy Buses", a utilitarian body on a three ton lorry chassis with solid tyred wheels. The department's next purchase would not be until March 1919 when ten ex-War Department chassis were secured.

Most of the smaller homes in the town would be heated by a coal fire in one of the living rooms. The fire would often be in a "Kitchener" a combined stove, oven and water heater. Many houses would also have a gas cooker and gas lighting would prevail. Fuel supplies held up well, due to the efforts of the Fuel Control committee, until the last year of the war when coal became more difficult to obtain. In August 1918 gas consumption was reduced by one sixth on pain of penalty if the required cut was not made. Demand for extra electricity for the war industries and the camps was to a degree balanced by the reduction in street lighting. The coal shortage was to become acute in the winter of 1918-1919.

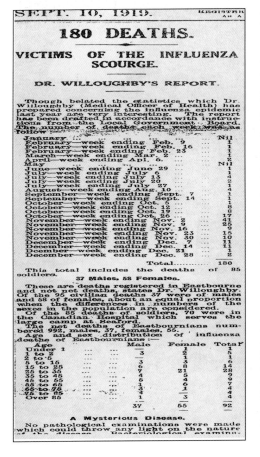

Health and Welfare

A snapshot of the nation's health was given by the call-up of men for the army. Of the six million men who were medically examined nationally for the services over one million were found to be grade C3, or unfit for active service. Farm labourers and miners were found to be the fittest with urban workers the least fit.

Since 1913, workers had been included in an insurance scheme known as the "Panel" which provided family doctor care, hospital care was provided for by payment according to means. The better off paid direct for all medical care. Eastbourne had 60

Doctors in 1914 but, despite a national call-up of doctors of 40%, the numbers listed locally in 1918 appeared much the same as 1913. Dr Willoughby the town's Medical Officer of Health was called up in 1915 and returned in 1919 in time to present the yearly report to the Council which detailed the figures for the influenza outbreak of 1918.

On 10th July 1918 the Eastbourne Gazette mentioned that the mess huts at Summerdown Camp had been closed because of an outbreak of Influenza. By the 30th October the schools were being closed as 11 Influenza related deaths had occurred within three weeks. The Eastbourne Chronicle of 26th October reported the death from Influenza of 10 year old Arthur Ellis of Winter Road.

On 25th October 1918 The Mayor of Eastbourne, Mr Alderman Charles O'Brien Harding, who was also a medical practitioner, sought to allay the resident's fears by stating that the number of deaths in recent weeks from respiratory infections were no more than previous years. No doubt the assurance was

NATIONAL REGISTRATION ACT, 1915.

For all men and women aged 18-65

made with the then current knowledge. In the weeks that followed the death toll rose dramatically so that by the end of the municipal year, 31st March 1919, the Medical Officer of Health Dr Willoughby's report revealed that 180 persons had died due to influenza, peaking with 41 deaths in the week ending 2nd November. The age range where most fatalities occurred was 15 to 35. Of the 92 Eastbournians who had succumbed, 37 were men and 55 were women. The remaining victims were servicemen from the aerodrome at St Anthony's Hill, Polegate Airship Station and Canadians from the Seaford camps who died in All Saint's Hospital. Some of the patients and nurses in the Central Military Hospital also died from influenza. The disease had appeared in the United States and India before it reached Europe. It claimed more victims than the wartime battles and struck hardest at younger people.

Infectious diseases, in pre-antibiotic days, were a serious threat to life. In 1914 the RAMC Headquarters at Dover asked how many infectious disease beds, for diphtheria, enteric and scarlet fever would be available, in Eastbourne for the army if the Newhaven infectious diseases hospital was full. The Council agreed to make 12 beds available. In 1916 Canadian soldiers from Seaford with infectious illness were sent to Eastbourne. Later in the war Acacia Villa in Wartling Road was also used. It was recorded that the monthly average number of infectious cases in 1917 was 21. Extra disinfection work for the army in 1914 necessitated the employment of an additional sterilizer attendant at the Downside sanatorium.

By August 1917 the increase in the number of cases of venereal diseases made necessary the setting up of a special treatment clinic. This followed an earlier refusal by both the Princess Alice and the Leaf Homeopathic hospitals to treat these patients. Proposals to site the clinic at the School Board's Dental Clinic met with opposition and eventually a wooden hut was provided at the rear of the Town Hall. The routine laboratory blood tests were carried out at the Royal Sussex County Hospital, Brighton at two Guineas (42 shillings) per patient plus a £50 general arrangement fee. More specialised Dark Ground tests would be referred to The London Hospital at three shillings and sixpence a time. The London was more competitive charging only five shillings for a blood test and three shillings and sixpence for a smear test. Patients who could benefit from treatment locally would be seen at the Town Hall clinic, otherwise the travelling expenses of the poorer patients would be paid. The heavy metal compounds, arsenic and mercury, introduced as treatments in 1910, were painful, unpleasant and prolonged. Antibiotics were 35 years away. A woman in 1918 was convicted of infecting soldiers and was sentenced to 6 months in prison.

Tuberculosis was another worrying health matter. A special sanatorium in Longland Road had been opened in July 1914 for such cases. It stood where Bodmin Close in Longland Road has been built. Rest, fresh air, sunshine and a good diet were the cornerstones of treatment. In 1917 nine new cases were being notified each month with 17 beds being occupied in October. Treatment was slow, months rather than weeks as anti-tubercular drugs had yet to be invented.

In October 1914 fifty-eight wounded Belgian Servicemen were treated at Wish Rocks and Urmston Red Cross Hospitals. By November 1914 Belgian civilian refugees were installed in Airlee and Merlynn in Devonshire Place, Upperton House, 20 Upperton Road, Four Winds, 27 Arundel Road and Halewood in Carew Road. Sympathy for the Belgian cause was expressed by Miss Farndell of Grange Corner who set up a fund to provide a field kitchen for the Belgian Army in March 1915. The refugees remained in the town until March 1919. Some had been self supporting but many had relied on relief provided by individual donors and the Red Cross.

Relief Funds were set up in 1914 to assist wives and families of soldiers and sailors but Government allowances were increased so little intervention was required. A War Pensions Act of 1915 required the Council to act as a Government agency to make the necessary payments of pensions, grants and allowances. A private soldier's widow would receive 13 shillings and ninepence per week. A Lieutenant's widow £2 per week plus one shilling and threepence weekly for each child to age 18 for boys and 21 years for girls. Boys over 16 years of age would have their earnings taken into account. By June 1916 these payments had amounted to £4,000 for a nine month period. By April 1917 there were 700 claimants. The council also paid for the storage of servicemen's furniture.

The Canteens

The YMCA provided beds at its main centre 23-31 Langney Road, where reading, writing and recreation rooms were also available. It

26   EASTBOURNE

Y. M. C. A.

Local Branch : **23 to 31, LANGNEY ROAD.**

President : Dr. AMBROSE EMERSON, M.A. (on Active Service).
Acting President : H. W. FOVARGUE, Esq.
Hon. Treasurer : J. LIEBENROOD, Esq.
General Secretary : HARRY T. WILFORD.

Membership open to young men over 15. Special Military membership.
A few Clubs still kept going. Bible Class on Sunday at 3. Hankham Mission every other Sunday. Nearly 200 members on Active Service.

WAR WORK.

FOR SERVICE MEN ONLY.   23 to 31, LANGNEY ROAD.

Canteen, Beds, Billiards, Baths, Reading and Writing Room, etc.

SPECIAL ! EVERY SUNDAY, TEA at 4.30
in Main Hall. SIXPENCE. Hymn Singing, etc.

Huts at Summerdown. Command Depot. Military Hospital.
R.A.F. Polegate.   Reading, and Games, etc., at Ordnance Yard.
Camps Leader : HARRY T. WILFORD.

established marquees and later huts at all the principal military establishments in and around the town, the Ordnance Yard, Whitbread

Hollow Camp, Summerdown Camp, the Cavalry Command Depot, Polegate Airship Station and Spots Farm Camp, Willingdon.

The first Canteen for troops was opened in 1915 in 7 Elms buildings 33 Seaside Road and continued to provide welfare facilities until 1919. A Union Jack Club for servicemen and their dependants was opened by Mrs Rupert Gwynne, wife of Eastbourne's MP, at 5, Windsor Terrace Seaside, in more recent years the home of the Charles Jewell youth club. An official opening took place in April 1915 when the wife of Admiral Jellicoe performed the honours. The club had a reading room with newspapers as well as books, a tea room and a nursery which boasted gas fires and a linoleum floor for hygienic reasons. Later a Girls' Union Jack Club opened premises in 1917 at 91 Seaside Road, opposite the Hippodrome.

The Churches of the town opened their halls for the recreation of troops. St Saviour's Church Rooms in South Street now the Masonic Temple became a canteen run by the ladies of the Church which offered not only refreshments but hot baths for the troops. Blackwater Road Presbyterian Church provided a canteen, the Methodist Mission Hall in Greenfield Road Old Town opened its premises for the benefit of the RAMC men at Summerdown Camp in 1915.

Private individuals took premises or used their own homes for canteens. Mrs H U Whelpton opened a canteen for troops at 58a Grove Road. A Home from Home Canteen in Church Street was run by Miss St Pierre-Bunburt, this was followed by Mrs Cameron's Blue Boys Canteen in Church Street. Sir Jesse and Lady Boot celebrated the opening of the cafe in their Terminus Road Store by offering free teas to Canadian soldiers in September 1916.

Strict Sunday Observance caused the Council to refuse permission for the Tivoli Cinema to open on Sundays for shows for the troops. This the cinema overcame by providing the Summerdown Camp with a projector and lending films free of charge. Polegate Airship Station also screened its own films.

Corporation's Contribution

Charitable causes in connection with the war mushroomed which led eventually in 1916 to the Official Registration of war charities. These good causes were often making requests to the Council to have reduced rate contributions in respect of properties occupied to house War Auxiliary Hospitals or for the accommodation of Belgian refugees and also to have the use of the Town Hall for fund raising events at half price. Such establishments often asked and were granted electricity supplies at half price. Belgian refugees, Blue Boys at Summerdown Camp and RAMC men at the Holywell camps were granted concessionary bus fares. Buses were supplied to take the Blue Boys from Summerdown Camp on afternoon drives on Sundays at a cost of one shilling per mile with voluntary drivers at the wheel. A request for a bus to transport the Summerdown Camp Band and its instruments to the Pier for afternoon concerts in the Pier Bandstand was refused. The camp also had a request for half price electricity refused. Troops in charge of an NCO were allowed to use Motcombe slipper baths at a special price of one penny, but towels were supplied at extra cost. Bowling rinks at Gildredge Park and sea front deck chairs were provided free for the convalescent soldiers.

Corporation employees who joined the forces had their army pay made up to their civilian job rate unless they were conscientious objectors who had been drafted into the civilian construction corps in which case they received nothing. By October 1917 war bonuses paid to Council employees totalled £7,476 and a further £3,834 had been paid to employees in the services.

The corporation had its own transport problems. By June 1918 an influenza outbreak had occurred in the corporation stables. Three horses had died. Of a total of 24 horses 12 were still ill leading to difficulties with refuse collections. Salvage of waste materials was promoted but with disappointing results, waste paper collected was often wet, only small amounts of rags and bones had been picked up and problems had been experienced with tin crushing machinery. An arrangement with a local mineral water company to take back bottles and syphons had foundered as the dustmen were traditionally "totting" (selling for gain) themselves which left nothing for the official scheme.

In August 1918 the Newhaven garrison commander under whose military jurisdiction Eastbourne lay, informed the council that sandbagged machine gun emplacements would be placed on the lower parade of the promenade. This was almost certainly a belated response to the German March offensive, on 12th August the German army was forced on the defensive and the threat of invasion receded. The emplacements would be located, by the south western outfall at Holywell, near the slipway at the Wish Tower opposite the Queens Hotel and at two places on Langney Point. Despite Council objections all except one on Langney Point were installed. Despite the warlike distractions on the seafront summer visitors would still be able to enjoy the hanging flower baskets which, it was claimed, took very little labour and there were plenty of plants in stock at the Council's nurseries to fill them. In July 1916 complaints had arisen about the dilapidated state of other sandbagged defences on the foreshore.

National Savings

National Savings by the purchase of War Bonds and Savings Certificates had been promoted through Banks and the Post Offices. In 1918 a more direct presentation of the savings message to the public was undertaken by having a rally and demonstration of a piece of military equipment to focus interest on funding the war. Lewes had a howitzer piece in a mock emplacement outside the County Hall. Eastbourne went one better by securing one of the new battle tanks for its rally in August. It was announced that the Tank, named Julian, would arrive on the 27th July by rail and would be kept overnight at Summerdown Camp.

There was a slight change in the plans when it was announced that Julian was too busy on the western front and that another tank named Egbert would come instead and stay for a week. Both Julian and Egbert were "male" tanks having six pounder guns, "female" tanks just had machine guns. Tanks were built to an eight foot wide railway loading gauge and would have their side gun turrets or sponsons removed for railway travel. The overnight stop at Summerdown Camp would enable the sponsons to be refitted. The tank arrived on 31st July and the next day drove on its own tracks down The Goffs to Terminus Road and along Cornfield Road to its parking place by the Princess Alice Tree. The Summerdown Camp Band headed the procession which also had 1,000 Blue Boys as a marching escort.

Tank Egbert at the Memorial tree Cornfield road *(John Palmer)*

An airplane flew overhead dropping leaflets. Permission had been given by the Council for a temporary wooden hut to be sited next to the tank to act as a bank selling National Savings. A number of rallies were held with patriotic speeches given by notables. Band concerts by the 13th Hussars of the Cavalry Command Depot attracted crowds to the event. Over the week £512,738 was raised for the war effort. Nationally, £2 billion of these bonds are still held today. Such is the damage of inflation that a £100 investment reached an all time low of £20 in 1975, now they are valued at £78 but at today's figure the pound is worth just five per cent of the original investment.

War Hospital Supplies Depot

The Red Cross provided bandages, splints, limb pillows and slippers to its own and other hospitals. The work outgrew 20 Upperton Road and was transferred to Knightsbook, 10 Grassington Road. By 1916 its volunteers had produced 72,000 items. The depot finally moved to Gonnville House, 8 Carlisle Road, temporarily vacated after reduced enrolment by Eastbourne College.

Other Shortages

In January 1915 the Council noted a shortage existed of scientific glassware, much of which had come before the war from the famous Jena glass working town near Leipzig. Glass tubes for generating X-rays, another import from Germany were in short supply until supplies could be obtained from the United States. Colour printing, dyestuffs and chemicals had long been German imports. For a seaside town another commodity, coloured postcards for the holiday trade which had been imported from Bavaria in quantity, also disappeared from the shops.

14. VICTORY and PEACE

By 1918 war weariness abounded, the Allies had suffered as many reverses as successes, and the cost in lives and treasure had been great. Russia, one of the Allies, had signed a separate peace treaty at Brest-Litovsk on 3rd March 1918. The United States had entered the war in April 1917 but by March 1918 only 500,000 US troops had arrived in France, but by July this figure would double.

Eastbourne Red Cross just older men and young boys 11-11-18

The ratio of Allied to German troops in France in 1917 was 3:2 but by 1918 with troop transfers from the Russian front it was now 4:3 in Germany's favour. The German High Command decided to launch a series of knockout blows on the allied armies before American aid arrived in strength.

Commencing on 21st March 1918 and ending on 17th July five massive assaults were made on different parts of the front. The 5th

Victory at De Walden Court Red Cross Hospital

British Army suffered the heaviest blow on the Somme in March yielding to a depth of 40 miles, The second attack came against the British at Ypres in April, during which Field-Marshal Haig issued the "Backs to the Wall" order.

The first Supreme Allied Commander, a Frenchman, Marshal Foch, was belatedly appointed. On 18th July the first successful allied counter attack was launched at Château-Thierry and this was followed on 8th August by the British and Empire troops' success at the Battle of Amiens. The German General Ludendorf described this as the "Black Day of the German Army". With deteriorating morale in Germany coupled with acute food shortages, the last 100 days of the war were characterised by a fighting withdrawal of the Germans on the western front and a disintegration of the armies of the Central Powers. At the end of

September, Bulgaria capitulated, in early October Turkey sought peace and by the end of that month the Austro-Hungarian Empire also sued for peace. By 3rd October the German Chancellor, Hindenberg, accepted the need for peace and by the 6th November a German armistice delegation had left Berlin for France. This series of events had been widely reported in the national and local press and the population of Eastbourne was thankful that on 11th November 1918 at last the war was over.

An announcement of the signing of the armistice was made from the steps of the Town Hall by the Mayor. Flags and bunting were flown everywhere. Good humoured crowds thronged Terminus Road where the Police and Special Constables kept order. Traffic became so congested that bus services had to be suspended. Members of the Royal Air Force and Canadian soldiers trundled up and down Terminus Road in lorries cheering and waving. South African soldiers gathered in Terminus Road near Cornfield Road forming a choir which rendered popular songs. People wore bows of red, white and blue ribbons and flags of the allied nations were flown. Mr Umberto di Giacomo at the Grand Parade bandstand cancelled the arranged programme of music and instead played selections of national airs and patriotic songs. Special thanksgiving services were held in all the churches. Rejoicing spread to the Central Military and Red Cross Hospitals as well as to the two main camps.

Lighting restrictions were eased and the blackout was relaxed. A rapid run down of war organisations occurred, and by Christmas most of the Red Cross Auxiliary Hospitals had closed. Early in 1919 the military establishments which had mushroomed in and around Eastbourne, Polegate Airship Station, St Anthony's Hill RAF Flying School, the Cavalry Command Depot had all ceased to be operational. The Central Military Hospital closed in July and the Canadian Hospital at All Saints completed its work in August but Summerdown Camp would continue into 1920. Between 1919 and 1922 local auctioneers would be kept busy disposing of equipment and buildings from all these establishments. In May concessionary bus fares for servicemen were withdrawn except for

Peace Day dancing on the Western Lawns

the Blue Boys. War trophies of captured enemy equipment were offered to the town. In February 1919 two machine guns and ammunition boxes were accepted. On 5th May the offer of a heavy German gun was declined but later that month the Librarian reported to the Council that a German ammunition wagon, flame thrower, gas mask, pump, stretcher and an anti-tank rifle had been received from the War Office. The Finance Committee was proposing to make arrangements for the accommodation of the items in the triangular enclosure near the Redoubt. The offer of a bombing plane had been refused, as also was an offer of an exhibition of Canadian official war photographs. A 105mm naval gun was declined over a £10 transport charge. By 1920 the German ammunition wagon at the Technical Institute had to be removed as it had become a danger to the boys who were climbing on it.

War Savings drives continued. The Council agreed in June to allow a hut for a savings bank and a mobile cinema to be placed at the Princess Alice tree in connection with the Victory Loan. Most large towns that had contributed to the drive for War Bonds were offered a tank as a memorial. Egbert, the tank which had come the year before to sell Bonds had been allocated to West Hartlepool. Eastbourne accepted the offer of another tank and on 20th September 1919 at 11.30 am the 26 ton tank arrived at Eastbourne railway station. It proceeded in procession on its own tracks via Grove Road to the Town Hall where it was welcomed by the Mayor. It then drove along Saffrons Road to Gildredge Park where a special concrete plinth had been laid as its permanent resting place. The presentation tank had fought at Ypres and Cambrai in 1917. In the years between the wars the presentation tank became neglected and after some debate the rusty relic of the Great War was removed in 1938 to participate as scrap metal in the re-armament programme for the Second World War.

The coal shortage became worse despite controls on its usage. Most households depended on one coal fire or kitchen range for warmth this would use about one hundredweight of fuel a week. In March 1919 the electricity works had two weeks supply of coal left. At the railway yard just 162 tons of house coal remained. The Electricity Department offered to release 50 tons and the Commandant at Summerdown Camp was asked to release War Department Coal. The Railway Company also offered 300 tons of its own coal. Coke, a by-product of gas manufacture, was in plentiful supply at the gas works. In May it was announced that the Defence of the Realm Acts would be relaxed to enable extra lighting to be used for Peace Day. At the same time The Board of Trade withdrew controls on street lighting.

War spoils, a tank arrives in Gildredge Park

Ex-servicemen

The Eastbourne Chronicle of 21st December 1918 reported the arrival home of the first batch of prisoners of war from Germany. Preferential consideration in local government posts would be given to ex-servicemen. A training post at the electricity works was offered to an Officer who had served at the Airship Station. Two other ex-officers were to be trained as sanitary inspectors. To help employment prospects the manager of the Electricity Department had agreed to conduct theoretical examinations in electrical engineering at the Summerdown

Camp. In January 1918, whilst the war progressed, a boot repairing course for ex-servicemen was started at the Royal Eastbourne Golf Club.

A Dugout Supper for ex-servicemen

The next year a caddies' training workshop was established for disabled ex-servicemen. Basketwork courses commenced at the Soldiers' and Sailors' Home in March 1919. In May 1919 the Council recorded that all lady clerks, bus conductresses and inspectors employed to replace men in the forces had been discharged. In December 1919 the Council received a request from the National Federation of Discharged and Disabled soldiers that jobs be found for 500 unemployed ex-soldiers, the Federation meetings took place at 112 South Street. The British Legion was formed in 1921 its meetings were held at 109 Pevensey Road. One of the features of the club would be the "Dug Out Suppers" which tried to re-create an air of authenticity for reunions.

Peace Day 19th July 1919

At the suggestion of the Mayor it was proposed that a dinner should be held for discharged ex-servicemen at the Devonshire Park. There was also to be a march past of ex-service men, a thanksgiving service, and sports events for servicemen's wives. A patriotic demonstration, sports and tea party for schoolchildren would be held in Gildredge Park. All the festivities were to be paid for by a grant from the rates of three shillings and fourpence in the £1 plus a call for donations. The balance of the rate contribution towards the Peace Day celebrations went to the Blue Boys' entertainment fund. The town's Hotels and Boarding Houses contributed generously to the widows' and orphans' entertainment and to fireworks and the Beacon on Beachy Head. In 1918 it was suggested that a roll of honour for the town's war dead was needed.

The Memorials

The townsfolk had paid a great price for victory, one home in ten had received a War Office or Admiralty telegram to tell of a loved one killed or missing, sometimes more than once. 1,056 local men and women of Eastbourne did not come home. The Eastbourne Gazette on 24th April 1918 suggested that a roll of honour for the town's war dead was needed. Two weeks later the Mayor asked that details of those lost should be sent to the Reverend Henry Plume who had volunteered to produce a record. A copy of the record card details of each man and woman, as provided by the relatives, may be seen in the reference department of the Eastbourne Central library.

Following the Armistice a meeting of influential members of the community was called by the Mayor to discuss the form a war memorial should take. The opinion favoured ex-servicemen's club in a town centre location. A Public Meeting in the Town Hall on New Year's Day 1919 failed to endorse the proposal. A wide range of alternative ideas were proffered such as an art gallery, council houses, a garden suburb at Summerdown and an organ for the Town Hall. Ultimately a War Memorial Committee was formed to make proposals and raise funds. The result was that a memorial costing £1,000 should be erected, and a garden suburb of houses for disabled ex-servicemen and their widows, should be built. The balance to be invested and the interest used to assist widows and dependants of the fallen. An appeal to all the 9,000 householders to give a donation coupled with an appeal in churches and places of entertainment produced the sum of £4,185 of which an amount of £1,578 was earmarked for the garden suburb. This latter sum was quite inadequate for the project. As a result the largest subscriber and four others asked for their money to be returned. This the committee did.

War Memorial dedication

It was decided to erect a memorial on the site of the Princess Alice Tree at the junction of Devonshire Place and Cornfield Road. A competition was arranged for the design which was won by Mr Henry Fehr, RBS with "Winged Victory" an angel in bronze on a granite plinth. The idea of inscribing the names of the fallen on the memorial was deemed impractical and instead the names were carved on oak panels fixed to the walls of the main staircase in the Town Hall. The tablets were prepared by a local firm, G Bainbridge and Son.

After the removal of the elderly Princess Alice Tree and some alterations to the street furniture, the War Memorial was ready for its unveiling on 10th November 1920 by General Lord Horne, GCB, KCMG, wartime commander of the First Army in France. Invitation cards printed with entwined Union Jacks were sent to all the relatives. Also invited were ex-servicemen, Royal Naval Volunteers, Territorials, Summerdown Blue Boys, Red Cross and St John Nurses, Scouts, Guides and Army Cadets from five schools. War orphans numbering 290, along with crippled and wounded servicemen were also present, the throng numbering close on 4,000 people.

The service was conducted by the Canon Streatfield, vicar of St. Mary's assisted by other clergy. Lord Horne released the Union Jack unveiling the statue, and the Eastbourne College Cadets sounded "The Last Post". The Mayor, Alderman Edward Duke, then accepted the memorial and oak plaques on behalf of the town. The ceremony concluded with the National Anthem and a march past of the organisations present. Lord Horne then went to the Town Hall to unveil the oak plaques of names. The following day the base of the memorial was surrounded by wreaths and flowers of personal tributes.

In 1919 the village spirit of Hampden Park had not been submerged in Eastbourne to the extent that it decided to have its own memorial to the men it lost. On 5th January 1920 the obelisk in Hampden Park on the west side of the Rosebery Avenue exit was unveiled by the Mayor.

During the debate on the town's main memorial controversy arose about the possibility of a multiplicity of memorials detracting from the main effort. This did not stem the tide, as applications had been made during the war to the Council for permission to place tablets on he front of the Town Hall to Bus Department employees who had been lost. Another application from footballers for a tablet also failed to gain approval. Churches remembered their lost members with plaques such as that at the Greenfield Road Methodist Church. Others erected memorial Halls as at St Mary's, Willingdon and Upperton Congregational Churches. St Saviours in South Street erected a cross of sacrifice in the grounds. Two memorials to Eastbourne's lost postmen are in the Southfields Road Public Office. For many years a commemorative memorial stone existed at the Gas Works for its lost men. The Eastbourne Schools also remembered their dead. St Mary's Boys had cause to remember the loss of the head teacher as well as former pupils. The private schools of which there were many in the town had their own memorials. The Ascham St. Vincent's school memorial arch still stands although the school is now no more whilst at Eastbourne College a phased extension plan funded by memorial donations commenced with the erection of the main hall and tower near the College Road entrance.

Many of the names on the private sector school memorials would have been of past pupils for whom the only connection with the town was the school. Most of the memorials over the years have been lost due to enemy action between 1939-1945 or redevelopment of buildings.

Eastbourne's War Graves

At the main entrance to Ocklynge Cemetery stands the Cross of Sacrifice designed for the Commonwealth War Graves Commission (CWGC) by Sir Reginald Blomfield. In contrast with the CWGC cemeteries overseas where the graves of the fallen are in orderly fashion the 130 of World War One in Ocklynge lie scattered singly and in small groups.

The Commission had its origins in France where a British Red Cross volunteer ambulance team, was led by Fabian Ware, a schoolmaster and administrator. In addition to caring and transporting the wounded, he became concerned that graves of the British soldiers who fell were often inadequately marked and the locations were not recorded. No military or government agency was charged with this responsibility. The Office of Public Works maintained some graves in the Crimea and had planted steel crosses on some of the Boer War graves.

CWGC marker in Ocklynge to Lt R R Swallow

From September 1914 to October 1915 the registration work undertaken by Ware was funded by the British Red Cross and then by the War Office. Eventually in 1917 it came entirely under the control of the Adjutant General with Ware still in command. The Commission's work was given impetus by a committee chaired by the Prince of Wales and extended to cover all the Empire's dead.

In the early days of the war repatriation of the fallen was possible, wealth and position enabling the exhumations to take place. This was exercised by the relatives of a grandson of Gladstone, a young Lord Lieutenant, to bring home his body. This practice was banned from April 1915 and from May 1916 private memorials were also forbidden. Thus equality of sacrifice was recognised, officer and enlisted man, rich or poor, were to be buried where they fell, their graves receiving identical marking.

The uniformity of interment however could not be enforced at home. Relatives of servicemen who died in the United Kingdom could have their lost ones brought to their home town for burial and could, if they so chose, have their own plot and monumental work. Three airmen, including a Brazilian and a high ranking army officer, all have private memorials in Ocklynge. The names of lost servicemen are on some private graves together with military embellishments such as rifles. These inscriptions are family memorials to men buried overseas.

Pvte E W Langford the first military funeral at Ocklynge

The criteria for a Commonwealth War Grave is that death should have occurred between 4th August 1914 and 31st August 1921, and be the result of wounds inflicted, accident occurring, or disease, contracted whilst on active service. The headstones are of either Hopton Wood or Portland Stone two feet six inches high by one foot three inches wide. They cost £3:9 shillings out of the total cost of £10 allowed per burial. The standard lettering was designed by Holmes Macdonald Gill and others. The inscription included the name, initials, rank, service number, unit name and badge. A maximum of three lines of 25 figures was allowed at the base for relatives'

tributes. The badges were roughed out from drawings using a pantograph machine and then with the lettering, were finished by hand carving. The main contractors for the Eastbourne headstones were Messrs J Andrews Ltd, of Willingdon Road and Messrs Francis and Sons Ltd, Carrara Wharf, Junction Road.

In Ocklynge there are 18 officers and 112 other ranks. The Army is represented by 107 burials, the Royal Navy by 9, the Royal Naval Air Service, Royal Flying Corps and subsequently the Royal Air Force by 14. Of the total of 130 burials, 42 have known local connections, another four men lie in Langney Cemetery, all with Eastbourne families. Between January 1916 and July 1919 there were 16,000 admissions to the Central Military Hospital (CMH) (formerly the Workhouse and latterly St Mary's Hospital), 100 of these succumbed to wounds and sickness, 17 of these are in Ocklynge. Two Women's Royal Naval Service stewards and two Red Cross nurses, from the CMH all dying from influenza, also rest there.

Other nationalities represented are South Africa with two burials from CMH patients who might well have come from the 600 strong contingent of "Springboks" in the Cavalry Command Depot in Victoria Drive. The eight Canadians from the CMH may have been too severe to be treated in the 16th Canadian Stationary Hospital which occupied All Saints Hospital from February 1917 to October 1919. Seven Australians and one New Zealander complete the Empire representation. Two United States airmen, one Belgian soldier and one Brazilian airman died in the allied cause. The Belgian's remains were repatriated after the war, the Americans were transferred to Brookwood Surrey and the Brazilian is still in Ocklynge.

The CWGC Cemetery Register sometimes provides additional information about each case, so we learn that a cluster of 13 deaths to respiratory causes coincided with the influenza pandemic at the end of 1918. Seventy young Canadian soldiers, from the Railway Construction Camps at Seaford, died from influenza in All Saints Hospital and were returned to Seaford for burial. Tuberculosis, malaria and poison gas claimed the lives of others whilst 12 were due to accidental deaths. Of the 14 Airmen from No 50 Training Depot Squadron, St Anthony's Hill aerodrome who lost their lives by accident, five remain in Ocklynge, three out of 14 lost from Polegate Airship station are also buried there.

The first military Funeral at Ocklynge took place in October 1914. Private Edward William Langford aged 24 of the 1st Battalion

Bedfordshire Regiment. A regular soldier having enlisted in 1907 he was recalled in 1914 as a reservist, he was with his unit retreating from Mons when he was wounded by sniper fire. The men were resting in an orchard at the time. His brother was a bandsman stretcher-bearer for the same battalion and picked up the wounded man, who was subsequently brought back to the Royal Herbert Hospital, Woolwich where he died. The brother was lost the following year at Ypres. The family home was in Wellesley Road. The sacrifices went across class barriers, Lieutenant the Hon. Germaine Frederick Freeman Thomas, Coldstream Guards, died of wounds on 26th September 1914, and Major Lord John Cavendish 1st Life Guards also died of wounds 24th October 1914.

Almost all were given funerals with full military honours with bands provided either by Summerdown Camp or the Cavalry Command Depot Victoria Drive. Firing parties were drawn from the Command Depot or the other service units stationed in the town. Funerals ranged from simple, with just a few relatives or comrades in arms, to civic with 2,000 people lining the route to Ocklynge as for the funeral of Lieutenant Colonel Oswald Fitzgerald, CMG, Lord Kitchener's ADC who drowned with his chief when **HMS "Hampshire** was lost in June 1916 on the way to Russia. Colonel Fitzgerald's next of kin, a sister, lived in Upper Carlisle Road. Sadly number 236 in the Eastbourne memorial register Stoker Bert Hookham, a driver for Elliot's Stores, and number 676 Stoker Percy Ramsay, of 10 Firle Road, whose bodies were never found, are listed as "Lost in HMS Hampshire". So both the highly placed and the less so were equal in sacrifice.

The Combatants, The Triple Entente or Central Powers

25-07-14	Austria attacks Serbia
01-08-14	Germany declares war on Russia
02-08-14	Germany invades Luxembourg
03-08-14	Germany declares war on France
03-08-14	Germany invades Belgium
05-11-14	Turkey joins in the war
02-10-15	Bulgaria joins Central Powers

The Combatants, The Entente Cordiale or The Allies

25-07-14	Serbia invaded by Austria
03-08-14	Belgium invaded by Germany
03-08-14	France at war with Germany
04-08-14	Britain declares war on Germany
06-08-14	Russia and Austria at War
12-08-14	Britain declares war on Austria
07-08-14	Montenegro declares war on Austria
23-08-14	Japan enters war on allied side
29-05-15	Italy hitherto neutral joins the allies
09-03-16	Portugal joins the Allies
01-04-17	United States joins the allied cause
26-10-17	Brazil joins the allies

SOURCES

Eastbourne Borough Council Minutes
Eastbourne Chronicle
Eastbourne Gazette
Eastbourne edition Sussex County Herald
Sussex Daily News

Eastbourne Bus Story, Spencer D, Middleton Press, 1993
A Military Atlas of the First World War, Banks A, Leo Cooper 1989
Battlebags British Airships of World War One, Mowthorpe C, Allan
Sutton 1995
British Regiments 1914-1918, James E A, Naval and Military Press 1998
Chronicles of the first World War, Randall G and Argyle C, Facts on File
1991
Cross and Cockade vols 4 1973, 5 1974, 15 1984, 19 1988, 20 1989
Dive Sussex, McDonald K, Underwater World 1989
Home Guard, Mackenzie S P, Oxford University Press 1995
In Good Hands, The History of the Chartered Society of
Physiotherapists, Barclay Jean, Butterworth Heinemann 1994
Shipwreck Index of the British Isles (South East), Larn R and B, Lloyds
Register of Shipping 1995
The Great War and the British People Winter J M Macmillan 1985
The Kitchener Enigma, Royle T, Michael Joseph 1985
The Pity of War, Nial Fergusson, Allan Lane 1998
The Unending Vigil, Longworth P, Constable 1967
War Magazines
    Springbok Blues, South African Red Cross Hospitals journal 1917
    Eastbourne Red Cross War Hospitals 1917
    The Ripping Panel, Polegate Airship station magazine 1918
    Closedown Souvenir booklet Polegate Airship station 1918
Summerdown Camp Journal 1915-1918

INDEX

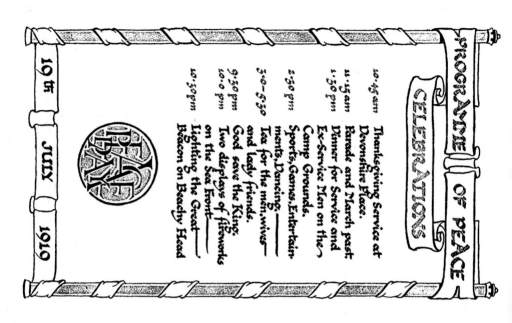

PROGRAMME OF PEACE
CELEBRATIONS

19th JULY 1919

PEACE DAY

10.45 am	Thanksgiving Service at Devonshire Place.
11.15 am	Parade and March past.
1.30 pm	Dinner for Service and Ex-Service Men on the Camp Grounds.
2.30 pm	Sports, Games, Entertainments, Dancing.
3.0–5.30	Tea for the men, wives and lady friends.
9.50 pm	God save the King.
10.0 pm	Two displays of fireworks on the Sea Front.
10.30 pm	Lighting the Great Beacon on Beachy Head.

COUNTY BOROUGH
OF EASTBOURNE

To ....

ON BEHALF OF THE PEOPLE OF EASTBOURNE, I tender to you on the day when we are celebrating the signing of the Treaty of Peace with Germany, OUR GRATEFUL THANKS for the arduous and valuable services which you rendered as a Member of His Majesty's Forces, in the Great War 1914–1919, and which have resulted in such a glorious victory.

1914   **1919**

Mayor